BEST OF IRELAND

Matthew Drennan

HERMES HOUSE

D1023833

Contents

Introduction

The Irish are a hospitable people, and sharing a meal with family and friends is an integral part of their lives in cities and villages alike. Food is unfussy, and dishes are often hearty and substantial. They all have one thing in common – the freshest and best of seasonal ingredients. The fertile soil ensures a ready supply of excellent beef, dairy products and vegetables. An island with miles of coastline and an extensive network of unpolluted rivers and lakes, Ireland is bountifully supplied with superb fish and seafood.

Potatoes are to the Irish what pasta is to the Italians and rice to the Chinese. In the past, the potato was almost all the poor had to eat; bleak necessity has given rise to a vast repertoire of tasty recipes using this versatile vegetable, including savoury soups, delicious side dishes and mouthwatering desserts.

This book includes all the classic dishes and traditional favourites, as well as many other recipes for all courses and occasions, from heartwarming soups to delicate desserts and delicious breads. A collection of side dishes using the potato is also included. Irish food is good food in the truest sense of the word and the best of it is very good indeed.

Ingredients

Meat & Poultry

Irish beef is world-famous for its superb quality. Both baby and yearling lambs are produced and most chickens and turkeys are free-range. Pork features less in Irish cooking, except in the form of bacon and gammon.

Fish & Seafood

Ireland is well-known for its excellent salmon. Other popular fish include plaice, cod and brill. Smoked fish is a speciality of some coastal areas, especially in County Cork. The choice of seafood is extensive – fresh mussels, clams, lobster, crab and prawns, including Dublin Bay prawns, are widely available. Oysters feature in the traditional Guinness & Oyster Pie, but this is no longer the inexpensive meal it once was.

Crab

Dublin Bay Prawns

Vegetables & Fruit

Potatoes are paramount, and floury varieties are the most popular. Waxy varieties are called "soapy" by the Irish. Cabbage probably ranks second in importance, closely followed by root

Cabbage

Carrots

vegetables, such as carrots, turnips and swedes. Other widely grown vegetables include onions, leeks, peas and beans.

Leek

Seasonal fruits are popular as summer desserts and include gooseberries, strawberries, blackberries, plums and raspberries. Apples and pears are also cultivated.

Apples

Dairy Products

Irish butter and cream have a well-deserved reputation and, even in these days of cholesterol awareness and low-fat cooking, are often included in a wide variety of dishes. Irish cheeses include Cashel Blue from Tipperary, Milleens from County Cork and St Killian from County Wexford.

Herbs & Flavourings

In many parts of Ireland, herbs, including garlic, grow wild. Parsley, chives, thyme and mint are the most popular flavourings.

Carragheen moss is a reddish purple seaweed harvested on the west coast of Ireland. It is rich in a natural gelling agent and minerals. It can be eaten as a

Above: The popular and versatile potato is used in many traditional Irish recipes.

vegetable like spinach, but is also available dried to a yellowish pink colour and used as a thickening agent. It is available from health food shops.

Young wild nettles are also harvested, especially in the spring. Only the tender young tips are used as the lower leaves and stems are too tough. If picking wild nettles, wear protective gloves and choose plants well away from traffic pollution.

Sorrel is another wild herb which is used in Irish cooking. It has a refreshing lemony flavour and can be used in salads, soups and sauces.

Drinks

Ireland has a venerable history of brewing and stout accounts for about half of all the beer sold in the country. Besides enjoying a convivial pint or two in the pub, the Irish also cook with it, classically combining it with beef and with oysters. The Guinness Brewery in Dublin is now world-famous. Other popular Irish stouts are produced by Beamish and Crawford and by Murphy's, both in Cork.

Techniques

Cleaning Potatoes

Locally grown potatoes from a farm shop or home-grown potatoes may still have some earth attached to them.

1 If the potatoes are dirty, use a small scrubbing brush or a gentle scourer to clean them. This will also remove the peel of new potatoes.

2 Remove any green or discoloured patches or black eyes carefully, using a sharp pointed knife or potato peeler, unless you are going to peel them after cooking.

Peeling Potatoes

Much of the goodness and flavour of a potato is in the skin and just below it.

1 Use a very sharp potato peeler to remove the thinnest layer possible in long even strips.

2 If you cook unpeeled potatoes and want to peel them immediately, hold the hot potato with a fork and gently peel off the skin.

Slicing Potatoes

Try to cut all the slices the same thickness so that they cook evenly.

1 Put the tip of the knife on the work surface or board first, then press the heel of the knife down firmly to create even slices.

Dicing Potatoes

If the recipe calls for dice, this means you have to be more precise and cut the potato into evenly shaped cubes.

1 Trim the potato into a neat rectangle first (keep the outside pieces for mash, or to add to a soup), then cut the rectangles into thick, even slices.

2 Turn the stack of slices over and cut into thick batons and finally into even cubes of the size needed for the recipe you are using.

Boiling Potatoes

1 Place the potatoes in a large pan and just cover with lightly salted water and a tight-fitting lid. Bring to the boil over a gentle heat and boil gently for 15–20 minutes. Boiling too fast tends to cook the potato on the outside first so it becomes mushy and falls apart before the middle is cooked.

2 Drain the potatoes through a colander and then return them to the pan to dry off.

Chopping Onions

Many dishes use chopped onions as an essential flavouring. Onions can be finely chopped easily and quickly using this method.

1 Peel the onion. Cut it in half and set it cut side down on a board. Make lengthways vertical cuts along it, cutting almost but not quite through to the root.

2 Make two horizontal cuts from the stalk end towards the root, but not through it. Cut the onion crossways to form small, even dice.

Steaming Potatoes This gentle way of cooking is particularly good for very floury potatoes and those which fall apart easily.

Chopping Herbs

Chop herbs just before you use them: the flavour will then be at its best.

1 Place the leaves on a clean, dry board. Use a large, sharp cook's knife (if you use a blunt knife you will bruise the herbs rather than slice them) and chop them until they are as coarse or as fine as needed.

2 Alternatively, use a herb chopper, also called a *mezzaluna,* which is a very useful tool for finely chopping herbs or vegetables and consists of a sharp, curved blade with two handles. Use the *mezzaluna* in a seesaw motion for best results.

Leek & Thyme Soup

A filling, heart-warming soup which can be processed to a smooth purée or served as it is here, in its original peasant style.

Serves 4

INGREDIENTS
900 g/2 lb leeks
450 g/1 lb potatoes
115 g/4 oz/½ cup butter
1 large fresh thyme sprig
300 ml/½ pint/1¼ cups
    semi-skimmed milk
salt and freshly ground
    black pepper
thyme leaves, to garnish (optional)
60 ml/4 tbsp double cream,
    to serve

3 Cover and cook for 4–5 minutes, until softened. Add the potato pieces and just enough cold water to cover the vegetables. Cover and cook over a low heat for 30 minutes.

4 Pour in the semi-skimmed milk and the seasoning, cover and simmer for a further 30 minutes. You will find that some of the potato breaks up leaving you with a semi-purée and rather lumpy soup.

1 Top and tail the leeks. If you are using big winter leeks strip away the coarser outer leaves before cutting the leeks into thick slices. Wash under cold running water.

2 Peel the potatoes and cut them into rough dice, about 2.5 cm/1 in, and dry thoroughly on kitchen paper. Melt the butter in a large saucepan and add the leeks and the thyme sprig.

5 Remove the thyme sprig, and serve, adding a spoon of double cream and a garnish of thyme leaves to each portion, if using.

Pea & Ham Soup

This substantial soup is based on the classic partnership of peas and ham and is packed with flavour. Delicious served with crusty bread.

Serves 4

INGREDIENTS
450 g/1 lb/2½ cups green
    split peas
4 rindless streaky bacon rashers
1 onion, roughly chopped
2 carrots, sliced
1 celery stick, sliced
2.4 litres/4¼ pints/10½ cups
    cold water
1 fresh thyme sprig
2 bay leaves
1 large potato, roughly diced
1 bacon hock
freshly ground black pepper

1 Put the split peas into a bowl, cover with cold water and leave to soak overnight. Drain.

2 Cut the streaky bacon rashers into small pieces. In a large saucepan, dry fry the bacon for 4–5 minutes, or until crisp. Remove from the pan with a slotted spoon.

VARIATION: The main ingredient for this dish is bacon hock, which is the narrow piece of bone cut from a leg of ham. You could use a piece of belly of pork instead, if you like, and remove it before serving the finished soup.

3 Add the chopped onion, sliced carrots and celery to the pan and cook for 3–4 minutes, until the onion is softened, but not brown. Return the bacon to the pan with the water.

4 Add the split peas, thyme, bay leaves, potato and bacon hock to the pan. Bring to the boil, reduce the heat, cover and cook gently for 1 hour.

5 Remove the thyme, bay leaves and hock. Process the soup in a blender or food processor until smooth. Return to a clean pan. Cut the meat from the hock and add to the soup. Season with plenty of black pepper and serve.

Yellow Broth

This famous Northern Irish soup is thickened with oatmeal which also adds to its flavour. It makes a hearty and nutritious lunch.

Serves 4

INGREDIENTS
25 g/1 oz/2 tbsp butter
1 onion, finely chopped
1 celery stick, finely chopped
1 carrot, finely chopped
25 g/1 oz/¼ cup plain flour
900 ml/1½ pints/3¾ cups
   chicken stock
25 g/1 oz/¼ cup medium oatmeal
115 g/4 oz spinach, chopped
30 ml/2 tbsp cream
salt and freshly ground
   black pepper

1 Melt the butter in a large saucepan. Add the onion, celery and carrot, and cook for about 2 minutes, until the onion is soft.

2 Stir in the flour and cook gently for a further minute, stirring constantly. Pour in the chicken stock, bring to the boil and cover. Reduce the heat and simmer for 30 minutes, until the vegetables are tender.

3 Stir in the oatmeal and chopped spinach and cook for a further 15 minutes, stirring occasionally.

4 Stir in the cream and season well. Serve with a grinding of black pepper.

Nettle Soup

A country-style soup which is a tasty variation of the classic Irish potato soup incorporating tender nettle tops. Serve with crusty bread.

Serves 4

INGREDIENTS
115 g/4 oz/½ cup butter
450 g/1 lb large onions, sliced
450 g/1 lb potatoes, cut into chunks
750 ml/1¼ pints/3 cups chicken stock
25 g/1 oz young nettle leaves
small bunch of fresh chives, snipped
salt and freshly ground black pepper
double cream, to serve

1 Melt the butter in a large saucepan and add the sliced onions. Cover and cook for 5 minutes, until just softened. Add the potatoes to the saucepan with the chicken stock. Cover and cook for 25 minutes.

2 Wearing rubber gloves, remove the nettle leaves from their stalks. Wash the leaves under cold running water, then dry on kitchen paper. Add to the saucepan and cook for a further 5 minutes.

3 Ladle the soup into a blender or food processor and process until smooth. Return to a clean saucepan and season well. Stir in the chives and serve with a swirl of cream and a sprinkling of pepper.

COOK'S TIP: Collect nettle tops in spring when the plants are up to 20 cm/8 in high. Wear gloves for this.

Celery Soup

Mild celery with a hint of nutmeg – this classic creamy soup makes a perfect starter served with wholemeal bread.

Serves 4

INGREDIENTS
1 small head of celery
1 onion, finely chopped
1 small garlic clove, crushed
few fresh parsley sprigs
2 bay leaves
1 fresh thyme sprig
600 ml/1 pint/2½ cups
    semi-skimmed milk
25 g/1 oz/2 tbsp butter, softened
25 g/1 oz/¼ cup plain flour
pinch of grated nutmeg
1 egg yolk, beaten
salt and freshly ground
    black pepper
chopped fresh parsley,
    to garnish
croûtons, to serve

1 Break the head of celery into sticks and wash thoroughly. Trim the root ends. Chop the sticks and leaves and put them into a large saucepan.

VARIATION: If you do not have a blender or food processor, pass the soup through a metal sieve, pressing the cooked vegetables through with the back of a spoon.

2 Add the chopped onion, garlic, parsley, bay leaves, thyme and just enough water to cover. Bring to the boil and simmer the vegetables, uncovered, over a gentle heat for about 35 minutes.

3 In a clean saucepan, bring the semi-skimmed milk to the boil. Knead the butter and flour together to make a roux and whisk into the hot milk until just thickened. Cook over a gentle heat for about 10 minutes, stirring occasionally. Pour into the celery mixture and cook for 5 minutes.

4 Remove the bay leaves and thyme. Using a ladle, spoon the soup into a blender or food processor and process for 1 minute, until smooth. Return to a clean saucepan and season well. Stir in the nutmeg and beaten egg yolk. Bring almost to boiling point, then serve garnished with parsley and croûtons.

Plaice in a Green Jacket

Fresh fillets of plaice, wrapped in lettuce, gently poached and served with a buttery white wine sauce.

Serves 4

INGREDIENTS
4 fresh plaice fillets, about 175 g/6 oz each
1 large head of round lettuce
2 shallots, finely chopped
1 bay leaf
300 ml/½ pint/1¼ cups dry white wine
275 g/10 oz/1¼ cups unsalted butter,
    softened, plus extra, for greasing
15 ml/1 tbsp snipped fresh chives
salt and freshly ground black pepper
boiled potatoes, to serve (optional)

2 Bring a large saucepan of water to the boil. Separate the lettuce leaves and drop them into the water for 1 minute. Remove with a slotted spoon and refresh under cold water. Drain well.

3 Lay out 3–4 leaves and put a plaice fillet on top. Season well and wrap the leaves around each fish. Top with more leaves, if necessary. Put the fish into a large buttered dish and pour in a little water. Cover with buttered paper and cook in the oven for 15 minutes.

1 Preheat the oven to 180°C/350°F/Gas 4. Using a very sharp knife, skin the plaice fillets. Insert the blade of the knife between the skin and the fillet at the tail end, then, holding the skin with one hand, glide the knife along the skin to remove the fillet.

VARIATION: This recipe would also work well with lemon sole fillets instead of the plaice.

4 Meanwhile, put the shallots, bay leaf and white wine into a saucepan. Cook over a high heat for 5 minutes, until reduced to about 60–75 ml/4–5 tbsp.

5 Remove the bay leaf. Whisk in the butter, a little at a time, until the sauce is smooth and glossy. Strain into a clean pan. Stir in the chives and season well. Do not boil. Lift the wrapped fish out of the dish and serve with the sauce and boiled potatoes, if liked.

Salmon with Sorrel

A luxurious, yet light, combination of flavours makes this dish delectable.

Serves 4

INGREDIENTS
225 g/8 oz fish bones
1 small onion, sliced
3–4 peppercorns
1 bay leaf
few fresh parsley stalks
300 ml/½ pint/1¼ cups cold water
25 g/1 oz/2 tbsp butter, melted
4 salmon fillets, about 175 g/6 oz each
120 ml/4 fl oz/½ cup dry white wine
300 ml/½ pint/1¼ cups single cream
75 g/3 oz fresh sorrel, washed
salt and freshly ground black pepper

1 Preheat the oven to 200°C/400°F/
Gas 6. Wash the fish bones and put
into a saucepan with the onion,
peppercorns, bay leaf and parsley stalks.

2 Add the cold water. Bring to the
boil, reduce the heat and simmer for
20 minutes.

3 Brush an ovenproof dish with some
of the butter. Add the salmon and
brush with the remaining butter. Bake
for 10 minutes, until just cooked.

4 Meanwhile, strain 150 ml/¼ pint/
⅔ cup of the stock into a saucepan.
Add the wine and cook over a high
heat until the liquid is reduced by half.

5 Pour in the cream and bring to the
boil. Reduce the heat and simmer
until the sauce just coats a spoon, then
season. Tear the sorrel into pieces and
add to the sauce. Cook for 1 minute.
Serve with the salmon.

Cod with Parsley Sauce

A traditional accompaniment for this tasty dish would be cooked cabbage.

Serves 4

INGREDIENTS

25 g/1 oz/2 tbsp butter, plus extra for greasing
4 cod fillets or steaks, about 225 g/8 oz each
1 bay leaf
6 peppercorns
small bunch of fresh parsley, stalks removed,
    leaves chopped
1 shallot, quartered
25 g/1 oz/¼ cup plain flour
300 ml/½ pint/1¼ cups semi-skimmed milk
salt and freshly ground black pepper

1 Grease a large flameproof casserole with a little butter. Lay the four cod fillets in the base, skin side down. Add the bay leaf, peppercorns, parsley stalks and the shallot.

2 Cover the fish with cold water. Bring to the boil over a low heat, then simmer very gently for 5 minutes.

3 Melt the butter in a saucepan, stir in the flour and cook gently for 1 minute. Strain the stock from the fish and reserve 150 ml/¼ pint/⅔ cup. Remove the fish from the casserole and keep warm. Gradually add the reserved stock to the flour mixture and continue stirring over a medium heat until smooth and thickened.

4 Gradually add the milk and bring to the boil. Reduce the heat and cook for 10 minutes, stirring occasionally. Add the chopped parsley, season and serve with the fish.

Wrapped Salmon & Rice

This dish is made with chunks of fresh salmon, combined with mushrooms, eggs and rice in light and flaky pastry.

Serves 4

INGREDIENTS
450 g/1 lb skinned and boned fresh
   salmon fillet
115 g/4 oz/1½ cups button mushrooms
6 spring onions
50 g/2 oz/4 tbsp butter
2 eggs, hard-boiled
175 g/6 oz/1 cup long grain rice, cooked
juice of ½ lemon
450 g/1 lb puff pastry, thawed
   if frozen
1 egg, beaten
salt and freshly ground black pepper
hollandaise sauce, to serve

1 Preheat the oven to 200°C/400°F/ Gas 6. Put the salmon into a saucepan with just enough water to cover it. Poach it gently for 10 minutes, until just cooked. Drain and leave to cool.

COOK'S TIP: To make hollandaise sauce, put 30 ml/2 tbsp each white wine vinegar and water, 1 bay leaf and 6 peppercorns in a saucepan and boil until reduced by half. Strain into a heatproof bowl set over a pan of gently simmering water and stir in 4 egg yolks. Remove from the heat and cook, stirring constantly, for 8–10 minutes, until glossy and slightly thickened. Season to taste.

2 Roughly chop the mushrooms and finely slice the spring onions. Melt the butter in a saucepan and cook the mushrooms and spring onions for 2–3 minutes. Place them in a bowl.

3 Flake the fish and add to the mushroom and onion mixture. Chop the eggs and stir into the salmon mixture with the rice. Stir in the lemon juice and season well.

4 Roll out the pastry to a rectangle 30 x 35 cm/12 x 14 in. Brush the edges with egg. Spoon the filling into the centre of the pastry. Join the edges and seal the sides and ends with egg.

5 Score the top of the pastry with a knife and brush with the remaining egg. Bake for about 30 minutes, until golden. Serve hot with hollandaise sauce, or leave to cool completely and serve cold.

Seafood Pie

There are as many variations of this dish as there are fish in the sea – use whatever is fresh and available.

Serves 4

INGREDIENTS
450 g/1 lb fish bones, cleaned
6 peppercorns
1 small onion, sliced
1 bay leaf
750 ml/1¼ pints/3 cups cold water
900 g/2 lb smoked haddock
225 g/8 oz raw prawns
450 g/1 lb live mussels, cleaned
675 g/1½ lb potatoes
65 g/2½ oz/5 tbsp butter plus extra,
    for greasing
25 g/1 oz/¼ cup plain flour
350 g/12 oz leeks, sliced
115 g/4 oz/1½ cups sliced button mushrooms
15 ml/1 tbsp chopped fresh tarragon
15 ml/1 tbsp chopped fresh parsley
salt and freshly ground black pepper
fresh tarragon, to garnish

1 Put the fish bones, peppercorns, onion and bay leaf into a small saucepan with the cold water. Bring to the boil, reduce the heat and simmer for 20 minutes. Remove from the heat and set aside.

2 Put the smoked haddock into a pan with water to cover it. Cover with a piece of buttered greaseproof paper and simmer for 15 minutes. Drain and cool, then remove the bones and skin and put the flaked fish into a bowl.

3 Drop the prawns into a pan of boiling water and cook until they begin to float. Drain and refresh under cold running water. Peel and add the prawns to the bowl of flaked fish.

4 Place the mussels in a saucepan with 30 ml/2 tbsp water. Cover and cook over a high heat for 5–6 minutes, until the mussels have opened. Discard any that have not. Refresh under cold water and remove the shells. Put the cooked mussels into the bowl with the fish.

5 Boil the potatoes for 20 minutes. Drain and dry over a high heat for 1 minute. Season and mash with 25 g/1 oz/2 tbsp of the butter.

6 Meanwhile, melt 25 g/1 oz/2 tbsp of the butter in a saucepan. Stir in the flour and cook for 1 minute. Strain the fish stock and measure 600 ml/1 pint/2½ cups. Whisk a little at a time into the roux until smooth. Cook over a low heat for 10 minutes.

7 Preheat the oven to 180°C/350°F/ Gas 4. Melt the remaining butter in another saucepan, add the leeks and mushrooms and cook for 4–5 minutes, taking care not to brown them. Add to the fish. Stir in the chopped herbs.

8 Pour in the sauce and fold together. Adjust the seasoning, then spoon into a pie dish. Spoon over the mashed potatoes and smooth level with a fork. Place in the oven and cook for 30 minutes. Garnish with the tarragon.

25

Prawns with Garlic Breadcrumbs

Fresh Dublin Bay prawns are a delight when smothered in garlic butter.

Serves 4

INGREDIENTS
32 Dublin Bay prawns
350 g/12 oz/1½ cups butter, softened
8 garlic cloves, chopped
30 ml/2 tbsp chopped fresh parsley
4 spring onions, finely chopped
15 ml/1 tbsp wholegrain mustard
115 g/4 oz/2 cups fresh white breadcrumbs
freshly ground black pepper
fresh parsley, to garnish
brown bread, to serve

1 Bring a large pan of water to the boil. Drop in the prawns. Cook until they float on top of the water. Drain and refresh under cold water.

2 Peel all but four of the prawns. Preheat the oven to 200°C/400°F/Gas 6. Place the butter, garlic, parsley, spring onions, mustard and plenty of pepper in a bowl. Beat until well blended.

3 Divide the peeled prawns among four individual ovenproof dishes. Divide the butter among them and spread it over the prawns. Sprinkle with the fresh breadcrumbs.

4 Bake for about 15 minutes, or until the breadcrumbs are golden brown. Garnish with fresh parsley and the unpeeled prawns, and serve with brown bread.

Hot Dressed Crab

This dish has topped the menu in Irish restaurants for many years.

Serves 4

INGREDIENTS
150 ml/¼ pint/⅔ cup milk
40 g/1½ oz/3 tbsp butter
15 ml/1 tbsp plain flour
350 g/12 oz fresh white crab meat
5 ml/1 tsp French mustard
275 g/10 oz/5 cups fresh breadcrumbs
30 ml/2 tbsp snipped
   fresh chives
salt and freshly ground
   black pepper
snipped fresh chives and chopped fresh
   parsley, to garnish

1 Preheat the oven to 200°C/400°F/ Gas 6. Bring the milk to the boil.

2 In another saucepan, melt 15 g/ ½ oz/1 tbsp of the butter. Stir in the flour and cook for 1 minute. Gradually whisk in the milk, a little at a time, until smooth and thick. Cook over a gentle heat for 5 minutes. Allow to cool.

3 Put the crab meat into a bowl with the mustard, 150 g/5 oz/2½ cups of the breadcrumbs and the snipped chives. Season and stir into the sauce.

4 Spoon the mixture into four crab shells or ovenproof dishes. Sprinkle with the remaining breadcrumbs and dot with the remaining butter. Bake for 20 minutes. Serve garnished with the chives and parsley.

Roast Chicken with Herb & Orange Bread Stuffing

This orange-scented chicken can be served with potatoes and roasted onions.

Serves 4–6

INGREDIENTS

2 onions
about 25 g/1 oz/2 tbsp butter
150 g/5 oz/2½ cups soft white breadcrumbs
30 ml/2 tbsp chopped fresh mixed herbs
grated rind of 1 orange
1.5 kg/3–3½ lb chicken with giblets
1 carrot, sliced
1 bay leaf
1 fresh thyme sprig
900 ml/1½ pints/3¾ cups cold water
15 ml/1 tbsp tomato purée
10 ml/2 tsp cornflour, mixed with
    15 ml/1 tbsp cold water
salt and freshly ground black pepper
chopped fresh thyme, to garnish

1 Preheat the oven to 200°C/400°F/ Gas 6. Finely chop one onion. Melt the butter in a pan and add the onion. Cook for 3–4 minutes, until soft. Stir in the breadcrumbs, fresh herbs and orange rind. Season well.

2 Remove the giblets from the chicken and put aside. Wash the cavity of the chicken and dry well with kitchen paper. Spoon in the herb and orange stuffing, then rub a little butter into the breast and season it well. Put the chicken into a roasting tin and cook in the oven for 20 minutes, then reduce the heat to 180°C/350°F/ Gas 4 and cook for a further hour.

3 Put the giblets, the other onion, the carrot, bay leaf, thyme and cold water into a large pan. Bring to the boil then skim off the scum. Simmer while the chicken is roasting.

4 Remove the chicken from the tin. Skim off the fat from the cooking juices, strain the juices and stock into a pan and discard the giblets and vegetables. Simmer for about 5 minutes more. Whisk in the tomato purée.

5 Whisk the cornflour paste into the gravy and cook for 1 minute. Season well. Serve the roast chicken, garnished with thyme and accompanied by the gravy, served separately.

Chicken, Leek & Bacon Casserole

A moist whole chicken, braised on a bed of leeks and bacon and topped with a creamy tarragon sauce.

Serves 4–6

INGREDIENTS
15 ml/1 tbsp vegetable oil
25 g/1 oz/2 tbsp butter
1.5 kg/3–3½ lb chicken
225 g/8 oz streaky bacon
450 g/1 lb leeks
250 ml/8 fl oz/1 cup chicken stock
250 ml/8 fl oz/1 cup double cream
15 ml/1 tbsp chopped fresh tarragon
salt and freshly ground
    black pepper

1 Preheat the oven to 180°C/350°F/ Gas 4. Heat the oil and butter in a large, flameproof casserole. Add the chicken and cook it, breast side down, for 5 minutes, until golden. Remove from the casserole.

2 Roughly dice the bacon and add to the casserole. Cook for 4–5 minutes, until golden.

3 Top and tail the leeks, cut them into 2.5 cm/1 in pieces and add to the bacon. Cook for 5 minutes until the leeks begin to brown. Put the chicken on top of the bacon and leeks. Cover and cook in the oven for 1½ hours.

4 Remove the chicken, bacon and leeks from the casserole. Skim the fat from the juices. Pour in the stock and the cream and bring to the boil. Cook for 4–5 minutes, until slightly reduced and thickened.

5 Stir in the tarragon and seasoning (it may only need pepper). Slice the chicken and serve with the bacon, leeks and a little sauce.

COOK'S TIP: Young leeks have a delicate flavour. If using older leeks, remove any woody core, and use mostly the white part.

Coddle

There are numerous variations of this traditional favourite dish, but the basic ingredients are always potatoes, sausages and bacon.

Serves 4

INGREDIENTS
4 back bacon rashers
15 ml/1 tbsp vegetable oil
2 large onions, chopped
2 garlic cloves, crushed
8 large pork sausages
4 large potatoes
1.5 ml/¼ tsp dried sage
300 ml/½ pint/1¼ cups chicken stock
freshly ground black pepper
30 ml/2 tbsp chopped
    fresh parsley, to garnish
soda bread, to serve

1 Preheat the oven to 180°C/350°F/ Gas 4. Cut the bacon rashers into 2.5 cm/1 in strips.

2 Heat the oil in a frying pan and fry the bacon for 2 minutes. Add the onions and cook for a further 5–6 minutes, until golden. Add the garlic and cook for 1 minute, then remove from the pan and set aside.

3 Add the pork sausages to the frying pan and cook on all sides for about 5–6 minutes, until golden brown.

4 Slice the potatoes thinly and arrange in the base of a large, buttered ovenproof dish. Spoon the bacon and onion mixture on top. Season with pepper and sprinkle with the sage.

5 Put the sausages on the top, and pour over the chicken stock. Cover and cook in the oven for 1 hour. Sprinkle with parsley, and serve with fresh soda bread.

COOK'S TIP: Virtually every Irish butcher has his own recipe for sausages. If you can find these kinds of sausages, you will certainly notice the difference. Alternatively, try some of the newer, more interesting sausages available in supermarkets. They won't be authentic, but will often taste delicious.

Boiled Ham & Cabbage

A no-nonsense dish that is full of warming winter flavours and very easy to make. This makes a substantial midweek supper.

Serves 6

INGREDIENTS

1.25 kg/2¾ lb ham, in one piece, soaked
   overnight (see Cook's Tip)
2 bay leaves
12 peppercorns
1 celery stick, halved
1–2 onions, halved
2 large carrots
1 large Savoy cabbage
salt and freshly ground black pepper
chopped fresh parsley, to garnish
boiled potatoes, to serve (optional)

1 Drain the water from the ham if you have soaked it. Tie the meat then weigh it to calculate the cooking time. Put the ham into a large saucepan and cover with cold water.

2 Add the bay leaves, peppercorns, celery stick, onions and carrots. Bring to the boil, reduce the heat, cover and simmer for 25 minutes per 450 g/1 lb plus 25 minutes.

3 Carefully lift out the ham and set it aside. Drain the cooking liquid into a clean saucepan and bring to the boil.

4 Meanwhile, discard the outer leaves of the cabbage. Tear the remaining leaves, including the heart, into pieces, discarding any of the tough stalks. Add to the cooking liquid and cook, uncovered, for 20 minutes, until tender. Taste for seasoning – you may not have to add any.

5 Serve slices of the warm ham on a bed of cabbage with a little of the cooking liquid poured over the top. Garnish with the chopped parsley and serve with boiled potatoes, if liked.

COOK'S TIP: It is always difficult to tell how salty a piece of ham is going to be unless you buy it from a regular source. If in doubt, soak it in cold water for several hours or overnight, changing the water at least once.

Irish Stew

Simple and delicious, this is the quintessential Irish main course.
Traditionally, mutton chops are used, but you can use lamb instead.

Serves 4

INGREDIENTS
1.25 kg/2¾ lb boneless lamb chops
15 ml/1 tbsp vegetable oil
3 large onions
4 large carrots, thickly sliced
900 ml/1½ pints/3¾ cups water
4 large potatoes, unpeeled and cut
   into chunks
1 large fresh thyme sprig
15 g/½ oz/1 tbsp butter
15 ml/1 tbsp chopped fresh parsley
salt and freshly ground black pepper

1 Trim any fat from the lamb. Heat
the oil in a flameproof casserole and
brown the meat on both sides.
Remove from the pan.

COOK'S TIP: Mutton – meat from
an animal over one year old – is still
available from some independent
butchers. It is stronger tasting and
darker in colour than lamb.

2 Quarter the onions. Add to the
casserole with the carrots and cook for
5 minutes, until the onions are browned.
Return the meat to the pan with the
water. Bring to the boil, reduce the
heat, cover and simmer for 1 hour.

3 Add the potatoes to the pan,
together with the thyme sprig and
cook for a further 1 hour.

4 Leave the stew to settle for a few
minutes. Remove the fat from the
liquid with a ladle, then pour off the
liquid into a clean saucepan. Stir in the
butter and the parsley. Season well and
pour back into the casserole. Serve.

Steak with Stout & Potatoes

This recipe uses the finest and most famous of all the Emerald Isle's ingredients: Irish beef, Murphy's stout and, of course, potatoes.

Serves 4

INGREDIENTS
675 g/1½ lb stewing or braising steak
15 ml/1 tbsp vegetable oil
25 g/1 oz/2 tbsp butter
225 g/8 oz baby or pickling onions
175 ml/6 fl oz/¾ cup stout
300 ml/½ pint/1¼ cups beef stock
bouquet garni
675 g/1½ lb potatoes, cut into thick slices
225 g/8 oz field mushrooms,
    sliced if large
15 g/½ oz/2 tbsp plain flour
2.5 ml/½ tsp mild mustard
salt and freshly ground black pepper
chopped fresh thyme sprigs,
    to garnish

2 Add the baby onions to the pan and brown for 3–4 minutes, stirring occasionally. Return the steak to the pan. Pour over the stout and beef stock and season to taste with salt and freshly ground black pepper.

3 Add the bouquet garni and top with the potato slices. Cover with a tight-fitting lid and simmer over a gentle heat for 1 hour.

1 Trim any excess fat from the steak and cut into four pieces. Season both sides of the meat. Heat the oil and half the butter in a large, heavy pan. Brown the meat on both sides, taking care not to burn the butter. Remove from the pan and set aside.

4 Add the field mushrooms. Replace the lid and continue to cook for a further 30 minutes. Remove the meat and vegetables with a slotted spoon and arrange on a platter.

5 Mix the remaining butter with the flour to make a roux. Whisk a little at a time into the cooking liquid. Stir in the mustard. Cook for 2–3 minutes, until thickened. Season and pour over the meat. Garnish with plenty of thyme sprigs.

COOK'S TIP: To peel the baby onions, put them in a bowl and cover with boiling water. Leave to soak for about 5 minutes and drain. The skins should peel away easily.

Guinness & Oyster Pie

Layers of crisp puff pastry encase a tasty rich stew of tender beef and fresh oysters. An ideal dish for cold winter evenings, served with fresh vegetables.

Serves 4

INGREDIENTS
450 g/1 lb stewing or braising steak
25 g/1 oz/¼ cup plain flour
15 ml/1 tbsp vegetable oil
25 g/1 oz/2 tbsp butter
1 onion, sliced
150 ml/¼ pint/⅔ cup Guinness
150 ml/¼ pint/⅔ cup beef stock
5 ml/1 tsp sugar
bouquet garni
12 oysters, opened
350 g/12 oz puff pastry, thawed if frozen
1 egg, beaten
salt and freshly ground
    black pepper
chopped fresh parsley,
    to garnish

1 Preheat the oven to 180°C/350°F/ Gas 4. Trim any excess fat from the meat and cut into 2.5 cm/1 in cubes. Place in a plastic bag with the flour and plenty of seasoning. Shake until the meat is well coated.

2 Heat the oil and butter in a flameproof casserole and fry the meat for 10 minutes, until well sealed and browned all over. Add the onion and continue cooking for 2–3 minutes, until just softened.

3 Pour in the Guinness and beef stock. Add the sugar and bouquet garni. Cover and cook in the oven for 1¼ hours.

4 Remove from the oven, spoon into a pie dish (about 1.2 litres/2 pints/ 5 cups) and leave to cool for 15 minutes. Increase the oven temperature to 200°C/400°F/Gas 6.

5 Meanwhile, remove the oysters from their shells and wash. Dry on kitchen paper and stir into the steak and Guinness.

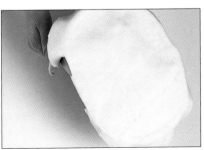

6 Roll out the pastry large enough to fit the pie dish. Brush the edge of the dish with beaten egg and lay the pastry over the top. Trim neatly and decorate. Brush with the remaining egg and cook for 25 minutes, until puffed and golden. Serve immediately, garnished with parsley.

Spiced Beef

Christmas in Ireland would not be complete without a cold side of spiced beef to see you through the holiday season.

Serves 8

INGREDIENTS
225 g/8 oz/1 cup sea salt
1.25 kg/2¾ lb silverside of beef or brisket,
    boned and untied
50 g/2 oz/½ cup brown sugar
2.5 ml/½ tsp ground allspice
2.5 ml/½ tsp ground cloves
2. 5ml/½ tsp grated nutmeg
1 bay leaf, crushed
15 ml/1 tbsp saltpetre
50 g/2 oz/1 tbsp black treacle
2 carrots, sliced
1 onion, quartered
freshly ground black pepper
pickles and bread, to serve (optional)

2 In a bowl, mix the brown sugar, ground allspice and cloves, nutmeg, bay leaf, saltpetre and pepper. Remove the beef from the salt and juices and wipe dry with kitchen paper. Sprinkle with the spice mixture and leave in a cool place overnight.

3 Lightly warm the black treacle and pour it over the spiced meat. Leave to marinate for 1 week, turning once a day.

4 Roll up the beef and secure it with string. Put it into a large pan of boiling water with the carrots and onion. Bring to the boil, lower the heat, cover and simmer for 3 hours. Leave to cool in the liquid.

1 Rub the salt into the beef and leave in a cool place overnight.

COOK'S TIP: Saltpetre is the common name for potassium nitrate, a powerful bactericide used for preserving raw meat.

5 Transfer the cooled beef to a board or a large plate. Balance another board on top, weigh it down and leave for at least 8 hours. Carve and serve the meat cold with pickles and bread, if liked.

Potato & Swede Stuffing

An unusual and delicious alternative to traditional stuffings. This amount is enough to fill a 2.75 kg/6 lb turkey.

Serves 8

INGREDIENTS
900 g/2 lb potatoes
1 large swede
115 g/4 oz/½ cup butter
4 streaky bacon rashers,
    finely chopped
1 large onion, finely chopped
1 large fresh thyme sprig
salt and freshly ground
    black pepper

1 Cut the potatoes into large equal-size pieces. Place in a saucepan and cover with cold water. Bring to the boil, reduce the heat and cover. Cook for 20 minutes.

2 Meanwhile, cut the swede into chunks. Place in a saucepan and cover with cold water. Bring to the boil, reduce the heat and cook for 20 minutes.

3 Drain both the potatoes and swede and dry out over a high heat for 1 minute, until all traces of moisture have evaporated. Transfer to a bowl.

4 Melt the butter in a pan and fry the bacon for 3–4 minutes. Add the chopped onion and fry for a further 3–4 minutes, until soft. Sprinkle over the thyme leaves.

VARIATION: Two sliced carrots can be added to the swede for the last 10 minutes of cooking.

5 Stir into the vegetables. Season well and mash until smooth. Use to stuff turkey and roasts as usual, or put into an ovenproof dish and cover with foil. Bake in the oven for the final hour of the meat's cooking time.

Champ

Simple but undeniably tasty, champ makes an excellent accompaniment to a hearty stew. Use a floury potato, such as King Edward.

Serves 4

INGREDIENTS
900 g/2 lb potatoes
1 small bunch spring onions
150 ml/¼ pint/⅔ cup milk
50 g/2 oz/4 tbsp butter
salt and freshly ground
    black pepper

2 Cut the green stems from the spring onions and set aside. Finely chop the remaining onions and put them into a saucepan with the milk. Bring to the boil and simmer until just soft.

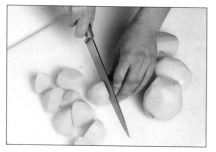

1 Cut the potatoes into even-size chunks, place in a pan and cover with cold water. Bring to the boil, reduce the heat, cover and simmer for 20 minutes, until tender.

COOK'S TIP: When buying spring onions, look for firm, white bases and undamaged green tops. They should be clean, with no sliminess, which indicates that they are no longer fresh. The mildest spring onions are the slimmest.

3 Drain the potatoes well and put them back into the saucepan. Return to the heat for 1 minute, until all traces of moisture have evaporated.

4 Mash the potatoes with the milk and onions and season well. Serve with the butter melting on top and garnish with the chopped green stems of the spring onions.

Colcannon

A famous and delicious southern Irish dish which is traditionally served with grilled sausages and bacon.

Serves 4

INGREDIENTS
900 g/2 lb potatoes
1 Savoy cabbage
50 g/2 oz/¼ cup butter
1 small onion, finely chopped
15 ml/1 tbsp chopped
    fresh parsley
salt and freshly ground
    black pepper

1 Cut the potatoes into equal-size chunks. Place in a saucepan and cover with cold water. Bring to the boil, reduce the heat, cover and simmer for 20 minutes.

VARIATION: Other varieties of green cabbage, such as pointed and drumhead cabbages, also work well in this recipe. However, do not use red or white cabbages, which have tougher leaves and require longer cooking times.

2 Drain the potatoes and dry out over a high heat for 1 minute, until all traces of moisture have evaporated, then mash them.

3 Meanwhile, bring another pan of water to the boil. Break off the outer cabbage leaves and discard. Tear the remaining leaves into pieces and cook in the boiling water for 15 minutes, until just tender.

4 Melt the butter in a large frying pan and heat until hot. Add the chopped onion and cook for 3–4 minutes, until just soft.

5 Add the mashed potato and cabbage and fry for 5 minutes, stirring occasionally until it begins to brown around the edges. Stir in the chopped parsley and season well.

Chocolate Carragheen with Irish Coffee Sauce

An impressive-looking dessert that is extremely simple to make. The secret ingredient is sure to keep dinner-party guests guessing.

Serves 4

INGREDIENTS
600 ml/1 pint/2½ cups full-cream milk
20 g/¾ oz carragheen moss
250 g/9 oz/1¼ cups sugar
115 g/4 oz plain chocolate
2.5 ml/½ tsp groundnut oil
90 ml/6 tbsp water
250 ml/8 fl oz/1 cup strong coffee
15 ml/1 tbsp Irish whiskey
grated chocolate and lightly whipped
    cream, to serve

1 Pour the milk into a heavy-based saucepan. Add the moss and 25 g/1 oz/ 2 tbsp of sugar. Bring to the boil. Reduce the heat and simmer for 15 minutes.

2 Meanwhile, using a sharp chopping knife, chop the chocolate into small pieces or grate roughly. Remove the milk from the heat and stir in the chocolate until it has all melted.

3 Strain the chocolate mixture through a fine strainer. Very lightly grease four teacups with groundnut oil, then pour in the chocolate carragheen. Chill until set.

4 Pour the water and remaining sugar into a heavy-based saucepan. Heat gently, stirring until the sugar dissolves. Remove the spoon and continue to heat the syrup until it turns a pale golden colour.

COOK'S TIP: It is best to use an Irish whiskey to make the sauce, as it has a distinctive flavour that is unlike Scotch, American or Canadian versions. Branded Irish whiskey is never blended and has to be matured for a minimum of five years.

5 Pour in the coffee and stir over a gentle heat until smooth. Remove from the heat and cool. Stir in the whiskey. Leave to cool.

6 Turn each mousse on to a plate and pour some sauce around each one. Serve decorated with the grated chocolate and cream.

Bread Pudding

This moist fruit pudding is delicious served hot or cold, cut into slices.

Serves 4–6

INGREDIENTS
450 g/1 lb stale white bread, thickly sliced
225 g/8 oz/1⅓ cups dried fruit
175 g/6 oz/¾ cup brown sugar
grated rind of 1 lemon
5 ml/1 tsp mixed spice
3 eggs, beaten
15 g/½ oz/1 tbsp butter
single cream and brown sugar, to serve

1 Grease a 20 cm/8 in round cake tin. Put the bread into a bowl and soak in plenty of water (about 1.2 litres/ 2 pints/5 cups) for 30 minutes. Drain off the water and squeeze out the excess moisture from the bread. Preheat the oven to 180°C/350°F/Gas 4.

2 Mash the bread with a fork and stir in the dried fruit, sugar, lemon rind, mixed spice and eggs, mixing well.

3 Spoon the mixture into the cake tin. Dot the top of the pudding with butter, then bake for 1½ hours. Serve warm or leave until completely cool and cut into slices. Serve with single cream and brown sugar.

Marmalade Pudding

Use a thick-cut peel marmalade for this delicious steamed pudding.

Serves 4–6

INGREDIENTS
115 g/4 oz/1 cup self-raising flour
pinch of salt
5 ml/1 tsp ground ginger
115 g/4 oz/1 cup shredded suet
115 g/4 oz/2 cups fresh white breadcrumbs
75 g/3 oz/6 tbsp dark brown sugar
175 g/6 oz/generous ½ cup marmalade,
    plus 60 ml/4 tbsp to serve
30 ml/2 tbsp milk
single cream and orange slices, to serve

1 Grease a 900 ml/1½ pint/3¾ cup pudding basin. Sift the flour, salt and ginger into a large bowl. Add the shredded suet, fresh breadcrumbs and sugar and mix thoroughly.

2 Add the marmalade and milk, mixing thoroughly to form a wet, dough-like mixture. Pour into the pudding basin. The mixture should three-quarters fill the basin. Cover with a double layer of greaseproof paper and secure with string.

3 Steam the pudding for 2½ hours in a double pan with a tight-fitting lid. Check the water after 1¼ hours.

4 Lift out the basin and remove the paper. Run a knife around the edge of the bowl, invert on to a plate and turn out. Warm the remaining marmalade in a small pan with 30 ml/2 tbsp water and serve with the pudding with cream and orange slices.

Pralie Apple Pie with Honey

This deliciously sweet apple pie is made with potato pastry which cooks to a thin crisp crust that melts in the mouth.

Serves 4

INGREDIENTS
225 g/8 oz potatoes
115 g/4 oz/1 cup plain flour
75 g/3 oz/6 tbsp caster sugar
2.5 ml/½ tsp baking powder
pinch of salt
2 cooking apples
1 egg, beaten
30 ml/2 tbsp clear honey,
   to serve

1 Cut the potatoes into even-size chunks. Put into a saucepan and bring to the boil, then cover and cook for 20 minutes.

2 Drain the potatoes and dry out over a high heat for 1 minute, until all traces of moisture have evaporated. Mash well in a bowl. Preheat the oven to 180°C/350°F/Gas 4.

3 Add the flour, 50 g/2 oz/4 tbsp of the sugar, the baking powder and salt and mix to form a soft dough.

4 Place the dough on a lightly floured surface and divide it in half. Roll out one half to a 20 cm/8 in round. Transfer to a lightly greased baking tray.

5 Peel, core and thinly slice the apples. Arrange them on top of the pastry. Sprinkle with the remaining sugar. Brush the edges of the pastry with beaten egg.

COOK'S TIP: For best results, use a variety of cooking apple, such as Sturmer Pippin or McIntosh, that retains its texture when cooked. Alternatively, use an "all-round" eating apple, such as Egremont Russet, Granny Smith or Jonathan.

6 Roll out the remaining pastry to a 25 cm/10 in round, then lay it over the apples. Seal the pastry edges together and brush with the remaining beaten egg.

7 Bake for 30 minutes, until golden. Serve hot in slices, with a little honey drizzled over each serving.

Carrot Pudding

A light steamed pudding made with grated carrot, plump sultanas and a hint of orange. The grated carrot makes the pudding beautifully moist.

Serves 4

INGREDIENTS
50 g/2 oz/½ cup self-raising flour
5 ml/1 tsp baking powder
pinch of grated nutmeg
1 carrot
50 g/2 oz/1 cup fresh white breadcrumbs
50 g/2 oz/½ cup shredded
   vegetable suet
50 g/2 oz/4 tbsp sultanas
grated rind of 1 orange
1 egg
120 ml/4 fl oz/½ cup semi-skimmed milk
caster sugar and whipped cream,
   to serve

1 Lightly grease a 900 ml/1½ pint/ 3¾ cup pudding basin. Sift the flour, baking powder and nutmeg into a mixing bowl.

2 Finely grate the carrot and add to the flour mixture. Stir in the fresh breadcrumbs, shredded suet, sultanas and orange rind.

3 Beat the egg and the milk together, then stir into the dry ingredients to form a smooth dropping consistency.

4 Spoon the mixture into the prepared pudding basin. Cover the basin with two layers of greaseproof paper, folded in the middle to allow room for expansion, and secure with string.

5 Steam for 2 hours in a double pan with a tight-fitting lid. Check the water after 1 hour and top up, if necessary. Remove the greaseproof paper and turn out the pudding on to a plate. Dust with a little caster sugar and serve with whipped cream.

Soda Bread

Fresh home-made soda bread makes the perfect accompaniment to hearty dishes, such as Leek & Thyme Soup and Coddle.

Makes 1 loaf

INGREDIENTS
450 g/1 lb/4 cups plain flour
5 ml/1 tsp salt
5 ml/1 tsp bicarbonate of soda
400 ml/14 fl oz/1⅔ cups buttermilk

1 Preheat the oven to 230°C/450°F/Gas 8. Sift the plain flour, salt and bicarbonate of soda into a large bowl. Make a well in the centre and pour in the buttermilk.

2 Using one hand, slowly incorporate the flour into the milk to give a soft, but not sticky, dough.

VARIATION: For good soda bread it's important to use buttermilk as its reaction with the bicarbonate of soda helps the bread rise. If you can't buy buttermilk, use sour milk or sour your own fresh milk with a few teaspoons of lemon juice.

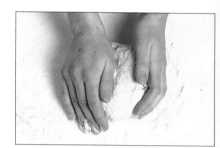

3 Turn on to a floured board and knead lightly for 1 minute, until smooth. Smooth and shape to a round about 4 cm/1½ in high. Cut a deep cross from one edge to the other. Place on a floured baking tray.

4 Bake for 15 minutes. Reduce the heat to 200°C/400°F/Gas 6 and bake for a further 30 minutes. To test if the bread is cooked, tap the underside of the loaf, which should sound hollow. Cool on a wire rack.

Barm Brack

This traditional Hallowe'en cake would once have had a ring baked inside.

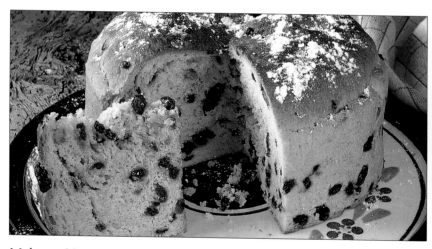

Makes a 23 cm/9 in cake

INGREDIENTS
675 g/1½ lb/6 cups plain flour
2.5 ml/½ tsp mixed spice
5 ml/1 tsp salt
10 g/¼ oz easy-blend dried yeast
50 g/2 oz/¼ cup caster sugar
300 ml/½ pint/1¼ cups warm milk
150 ml/¼ pint/⅔ cup warm water
50 g/2 oz/4 tbsp butter, softened
50 g/2 oz/4 tbsp currants
225 g/8 oz/1½ cups sultanas
50 g/2 oz/5 tbsp chopped peel
milk or syrup, to glaze
icing sugar, to decorate

1 Grease a 23 cm/9 in round cake tin. Sift the flour, mixed spice and salt together. Stir in the yeast and 15 ml/1 tbsp of the sugar.

2 Make a well, then pour in the milk and water and mix to a dough. Transfer to a floured board and knead until smooth and no longer sticky. Place in a clean bowl, cover with clear film and leave in a warm place for 1 hour, until well risen and doubled in size.

3 Add the butter, currants, sultanas and chopped peel and work into the dough. Return to the bowl and cover. Leave for another 30 minutes. Preheat the oven to 200°C/400°F/Gas 6.

4 Fit the dough into the tin and leave to rise to the top. Brush with milk or syrup and bake for 15 minutes. Cover with foil. Reduce the heat to 180°C/350°F/Gas 4 and bake for 45 minutes. Dust with icing sugar.

Irish Coffee

This classic Irish beverage is included in the dessert section because, as the Irish say, "there's eating and drinking in it!"

Makes 4

INGREDIENTS
20 ml/4 tsp granulated sugar
600 ml/1 pint/2½ cups strong hot coffee
4 measures Irish whiskey
300 ml/½ pint/1¼ cups thick double cream

1 Divide the granulated sugar among four stemmed, heatproof glasses. Put a metal teaspoon in each glass.

2 Carefully pour in the hot coffee and stir to dissolve the sugar.

3 Stir a measure of whiskey into each glass. Remove the teaspoon and hold it upside-down over the glass.

4 Slowly pour the double cream over the back of the spoon on to the hot coffee so that it floats on the surface. Serve at once.

The edition published by Hermes House

Hermes House is an imprint of Anness Publishing Limited,
Hermes House,
88–89 Blackfriars Road,
London SE1 8HA

Publisher: Joanna Lorenz
Editor: Valerie Ferguson
Series Designer: Bobbie Colgate Stone
Designer: Andrew Heath
Editorial Reader: Marion Wilson
Production Controller: Joanna King
Recipes contributed by: Matthew Drennan
Photography: Thomas Odulate

3 5 7 9 10 8 6 4 2

Notes:
For all recipes, quantities are given in both metric and imperial measures and, where appropriate, measures are also given in standard cups and spoons.
Follow one set, but not a mixture, because they are not interchangeable.

Standard spoon and cup measures are level.

1 tsp = 5 ml   1 tbsp = 15 ml   1 cup = 250 ml/8 fl oz

Australian standard tablespoons are 20 ml.
Australian readers should use 3 tsp in place of 1 tbsp for measuring small quantities of gelatine, cornflour, salt, etc.

Medium eggs are used unless otherwise stated.

Printed in China

Ingredients

Many of the ingredients needed to create an authentic Thai meal at home are now widely available in supermarkets; others can be obtained from Asian and specialist shops.

Bamboo Shoots

The edible young shoots of the bamboo plant. When buying canned shoots, look for the whole ones as they seem to be of better quality than the ready-sliced canned shoots.

Banana Leaves

Glossy, dark green leaves of the banana trees are used to line steamers or to wrap foods such as fish before grilling or baking. They impart a slight flavour of fine tea.

Basil

The herb sweet basil is well known in Mediterranean cooking; in Thailand the hotter, slightly medicinal-tasting Thai basil is used frequently.

Beancurd (Tofu)

Made from soya beans, this is sold in blocks packed in water and is available fresh, smoked and dried.

Bean Sauce

Made from salted, fermented soya beans, this sauce is a popular flavouring agent in Asian dishes.

Blachan

A strong-smelling, firm paste made of fermented shrimps, used as a flavouring. To prepare blachan, wrap a piece in foil and dry fry over a gentle heat for 5 minutes, turning occasionally.

Chilli

The small red and green fresh chillies known as Thai or bird's eye chillies are extremely hot. Larger varieties are in fact slightly milder.

Coconut Milk

This unsweetened liquid, made from grated coconut flesh and water, is an essential ingredient of many Thai dishes. It is available in cans, compressed blocks and as a powder.

Coriander

The leaves and seeds of this plant are among the most essential flavourings in Thai cooking. The root is also used.

Fish Sauce

The most commonly used flavouring ingredient in Thai food. It is made from salted anchovies and has a strong, salty flavour.

Galangal

This looks similar to fresh root ginger and is prepared in the same way. It has a wonderful sharp, lemony taste.

Garlic

Indispensable in Thai cooking. Pickled garlic, available in jars, is also used.

Ginger

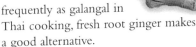

Fresh root ginger should be peeled and chopped or crushed before cooking. Though not used as frequently as galangal in Thai cooking, fresh root ginger makes a good alternative.

Kaffir Lime

The fruit is similar to the common lime, but has a knobbly skin. The glossy, dark green leaves impart a pungent lemon-lime flavour to dishes.

Lemon Grass

Similar to a spring onion, this has long, pale green stalks and a bulbous end. It has a woody texture and an aromatic lemon scent. Unless finely chopped, it is always removed from a dish before serving because it is so fibrous.

Tamarind

An acidic tropical fruit that resembles a bean pod, usually sold dried or pulped. To make tamarind juice, soak 25 g/ 1 oz dried tamarind in 150 ml/¼ pint/ ⅔ cup warm water for 10 minutes.

Basic Recipes

These pastes are used continually in Thai cooking. Make up double the quantity and refrigerate for up to 4 weeks, or freeze what is not required.

Red Curry Paste

This paste is used in Thai meat, poultry and vegetable dishes.

Makes about 175 g/6 oz

INGREDIENTS
10 red chillies, seeded and sliced,
   or 7.5 ml/1½ tsp chilli powder
115 g/4 oz dark red onions or shallots, sliced
4 garlic cloves
3 lemon grass stalks, lower part of stem
   sliced and bruised
1 cm/½ in piece galangal, peeled, sliced
   and bruised
4 fresh coriander sprigs, stems only
15–30 ml/1–2 tbsp groundnut oil
5 ml/1 tsp grated dried citrus peel
1 cm/½ in cube blachan, prepared
15 ml/1 tbsp coriander seeds
10 ml/2 tsp cumin seeds
5 ml/1 tsp salt

1 Pound the chillies or chilli powder, onions or shallots, garlic, lemon grass, galangal and the stems from the coriander sprigs in a mortar to a paste, gradually adding the oil. Add the dried citrus peel and blachan.

2 Dry fry the coriander and cumin seeds, then turn them into a clean mortar and grind them to a powder. Add the ground spices to the paste with the salt and mix well.

Green Curry Paste

Make this using the same ingredients as for red curry paste, but with green chillies in place of the red chillies, white onion instead of a red one, and adding the leaves from the coriander to strengthen the colour.

Preparing Lemon Grass

Use the whole stem and remove it from the dish after cooking, or chop the stem finely.

1 Trim the end of the stem and trim off the top, until you are left with about 10 cm/4 in.

2 Split in half lengthways and finely chop or, if the bulb is particularly fresh, thinly slice. Use as required.

Nam Prik Sauce

The most famous of all Thai sauces, this can be served on its own or stirred into plain cooked rice.

Makes 275 g/10 oz

INGREDIENTS

50 g/2 oz/1 cup dried shrimps, soaked in
    water for 15 minutes and drained
1 cm/½ in cube blachan, prepared
3–4 garlic cloves, crushed
3–4 red chillies, seeded and sliced
50 g/2 oz peeled cooked prawns (optional)
a few sprigs of fresh coriander
8–10 tiny baby aubergines, stalks removed
45–60 ml/3–4 tbsp lemon or lime juice
30 ml/2 tbsp fish sauce, or to taste
15 ml/1 tbsp brown sugar, or to taste

1 Pound the shrimps, blachan, garlic and sliced chillies together in a mortar. Add the fresh cooked prawns, if using, and the coriander. Pound the ingredients again until well combined.

2 Add the aubergines to the mortar and pound into the sauce. Add the lemon or lime juice, fish sauce and sugar to taste, plus a little water if a thinner sauce is required.

Preparing Chillies

Fresh chillies add a distinctive flavour, but remove the seeds before slicing the flesh as they are fiery-hot.

1 Always protect your hands when preparing fresh chillies, as the juice can irritate the skin; wear rubber gloves and be careful never to rub your eyes after handling chillies. Halve the chilli lengthways and remove and discard the cluster of seeds.

2 Slice and finely chop the chilli flesh and use as required. Wash the knife and chopping board thoroughly in plenty of hot, soapy water. Always wash your hands immediately after preparing chillies, even if you have been wearing rubber gloves.

Fish Cakes with Cucumber Relish

These wonderful small fish cakes are a very familiar and popular appetizer. They are usually served with Thai beer.

Makes about 12

INGREDIENTS
300 g/11 oz white fish fillet, such as cod,
    cut into chunks
30 ml/2 tbsp red curry paste
1 egg
30 ml/2 tbsp fish sauce
5 ml/1 tsp sugar
30 ml/2 tbsp cornflour
3 kaffir lime leaves, shredded
15 ml/1 tbsp chopped fresh coriander
50 g/2 oz green beans, finely sliced
oil, for frying
Chinese mustard cress, to garnish

FOR THE CUCUMBER RELISH
60 ml/4 tbsp Thai coconut or rice vinegar
60 ml/4 tbsp water
50 g/2 oz sugar
1 pickled garlic head
1 cucumber, quartered and sliced
4 shallots, finely sliced
15 ml/1 tbsp finely chopped fresh root ginger

1 To make the cucumber relish, bring the vinegar, water and sugar to the boil. Stir until the sugar dissolves, then remove from the heat and cool.

2 Combine the rest of the relish ingredients in a bowl and pour over the vinegar mixture.

3 Put the fish, curry paste and egg in a food processor and process well. Transfer the mixture to a bowl, add the rest of the ingredients, except the oil and garnish, and mix well.

4 Mould and shape the mixture into cakes about 5 cm/2 in in diameter and 5 mm/¼ in thick.

5 Heat the oil in a wok or deep-fat fryer. Fry the fish cakes for 4-5 minutes. Remove and drain. Garnish with Chinese mustard cress and serve with the cucumber relish.

Steamed Seafood Packets

Very neat and delicate, these little steamed packets make an excellent starter or a light and unusual lunch dish.

Serves 4

INGREDIENTS
225 g/8 oz crab meat
50 g/2 oz shelled prawns, chopped
6 water chestnuts, chopped
30 ml/2 tbsp chopped bamboo shoots
15 ml/1 tbsp chopped spring onion
5 ml/1 tsp chopped fresh root ginger
15 ml/1 tbsp soy sauce
15 ml/1 tbsp fish sauce
12 rice sheets
banana leaves, or foil
oil, for brushing
2 spring onions, shredded, 2 red chillies, seeded and sliced, and fresh coriander leaves, to garnish

1 Combine the crab meat, chopped prawns, chestnuts, bamboo shoots, spring onion and ginger in a bowl. Mix well, then add the soy sauce and fish sauce. Stir to blend.

2 Take a single rice sheet and dip it in warm water. Place it on a clean flat surface and leave it for a few seconds to soften.

COOK'S TIP: The seafood packets will spread out when steamed, so be sure to space them well apart to prevent them sticking together.

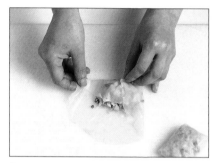

3 Place a spoonful of the seafood mixture in the centre of the sheet and fold into a square packet. Repeat with the rest of the rice sheets and seafood mixture.

4 Use banana leaves or foil to line a steamer, then brush with oil. Place the packets, seam-side down, on the leaves or foil and steam over a high heat for 6–8 minutes or until the filling is cooked. Transfer to a plate, garnish with shredded spring onions, sliced chillies and coriander leaves and serve.

Rice Cakes with Spicy Dipping Sauce

Rice cakes are a classic Thai appetizer. They are easy to prepare and make a useful standby since they keep well in an airtight box.

Serves 4–6

INGREDIENTS
175 g/6 oz/1 cup jasmine rice
350 ml/12 fl oz/1½ cups water
oil, for frying and greasing

FOR THE SPICY DIPPING SAUCE
6–8 dried chillies, seeded and soaked in
　warm water for 20 minutes
2.5 ml/½ tsp salt
2 shallots, chopped
2 garlic cloves, chopped
4 coriander roots
10 white peppercorns
250 ml/8 fl oz/1 cup
　coconut milk
5 ml/1 tsp shrimp paste
115 g/4 oz minced pork
115 g/4 oz cherry tomatoes, chopped
15 ml/1 tbsp fish sauce
15 ml/1 tbsp palm sugar or soft dark
　brown sugar
30 ml/2 tbsp tamarind juice
30 ml/2 tbsp coarsely chopped
　roasted peanuts
2 spring onions, finely chopped

1 Drain the chillies and crush in a mortar with the salt. Add the chopped shallots, garlic, coriander roots and peppercorns and pound the mixture into a coarse paste.

2 Boil the coconut milk until it begins to separate. Add the chilli paste. Cook for 2–3 minutes until it is fragrant. Stir in the shrimp paste. Cook for another minute.

3 Add the minced pork, stirring to break up any lumps. Cook for about 5–10 minutes. Add the tomatoes, fish sauce, sugar and tamarind juice. Simmer until the sauce thickens. Stir in the peanuts and spring onions. Remove from the heat and leave to cool.

4 Wash the rice well. Bring to the boil with the water, then cover and leave to simmer for about 15 minutes. Turn out on to a lightly greased tray and press down. Leave overnight in a very low oven until the rice is completely dry and firm.

5 Remove the rice from the tray and break into bite-size pieces. Heat the oil and deep fry the rice cakes in batches for about 1 minute, until they puff up, taking care not to over-brown them. Drain and serve with the dipping sauce.

Spring Rolls

These crunchy spring rolls are as popular in Thai cuisine as they are in Chinese, and have a delicious pork, prawn and garlic filling.

Makes about 24

INGREDIENTS
4–6 dried Chinese mushrooms, soaked
50 g/2 oz bean thread
    noodles, soaked
oil, for frying
2 garlic cloves, chopped
2 red chillies, seeded and chopped
225 g/8 oz minced pork
50 g/2 oz chopped cooked prawns
30 ml/2 tbsp fish sauce
5 ml/1 tsp sugar
1 carrot, finely shredded
50 g/2 oz bamboo shoots, chopped
50 g/2 oz beansprouts
2 spring onions, chopped
15 ml/1 tbsp chopped fresh coriander
30 ml/2 tbsp flour
24 x 15 cm/6 in square spring
    roll wrappers
freshly ground black pepper
spring onions, carrots and red chillies,
    cut in slivers, to garnish
sweet chilli sauce, to serve (optional)

1 Drain and chop the mushrooms. Cut the drained noodles into short lengths, about 5 cm/2 in.

2 Heat 30 ml/2 tbsp oil in a wok or frying pan, add the chopped garlic and chillies and fry for 30 seconds. Add the minced pork, stirring until the meat is browned.

3 Add the noodles, mushrooms and prawns to the wok or frying pan. Season with fish sauce, sugar and freshly ground black pepper. Tip the mixture into a bowl. Mix in the shredded carrot, bamboo shoots, beansprouts, spring onions and chopped fresh coriander until well combined.

4 Mix the flour with a little water to make a paste for sealing the rolls. Place a spoonful of the pork mixture in the centre of a spring roll wrapper. Turn the bottom edge of the wrapper over to cover the filling, then fold in the left and right sides.

5 Roll the wrapper up almost to the top edge. Brush the top edge with flour paste and seal. Repeat with the rest of the spring roll wrappers. Heat some oil and fry the spring rolls a few at a time until crisp and golden brown. Drain. Garnish with slivers of spring onion, carrot and red chilli. Serve with sweet chilli sauce for dipping, if liked.

Spinach & Beancurd Soup

An extremely delicate and mild-flavoured soup that can be a useful choice of dish with which to counterbalance the heat from a hot Thai curry.

Serves 4–6

INGREDIENTS
30 ml/2 tbsp dried shrimps
1 litre/1¾ pints/4 cups
   chicken stock
225 g/8 oz fresh beancurd (tofu),
   drained and cut into
   2 cm/¾ in cubes
30 ml/2 tbsp fish sauce
350 g/12 oz spinach
freshly ground black pepper
2 spring onions, finely sliced,
   to garnish

1 Rinse and drain the dried shrimps. Combine the shrimps with the chicken stock in a large saucepan and bring the stock to the boil.

COOK'S TIP: This soup is especially delicious made from home-made chicken stock. Make up a large batch and store the rest in the freezer.

2 Add the beancurd and simmer for about 5 minutes. Season with fish sauce and black pepper to taste.

3 Wash the spinach thoroughly in several changes of water and drain well. Tear the leaves into bite-size pieces and add to the soup. Leave the soup to cook for another 1–2 minutes.

4 Remove from the heat, pour into soup bowls, sprinkle over the finely sliced spring onions and serve.

Chicken & Coconut Soup

This soup is rich with coconut milk and aromatic Thai spices.

Serves 4–6

INGREDIENTS
750 ml/1¼ pints/3 cups coconut milk
475 ml/16 fl oz/2 cups chicken stock
4 lemon grass stalks, bruised and chopped
2.5 cm/1 in piece galangal, thinly sliced
10 black peppercorns, crushed
10 kaffir lime leaves, torn
300 g/11 oz boneless chicken, cut into strips
115 g/4 oz/1½ cups button mushrooms
50 g/2 oz baby sweetcorn
60 ml/4 tbsp lime juice
45 ml/3 tbsp fish sauce, or to taste
chopped red chillies, spring onions and fresh
    coriander leaves, to garnish

1 Bring the coconut milk and chicken stock to the boil. Add the lemon grass, galangal, peppercorns and half the kaffir lime leaves, reduce the heat and simmer gently for 10 minutes.

2 Strain the stock into a clean pan. Return to the heat, then add the chicken, mushrooms and sweetcorn. Cook for about 5–7 minutes or until the chicken is cooked.

3 Stir in the lime juice, fish sauce to taste and the rest of the lime leaves. Serve hot, garnished with red chillies, spring onions and coriander.

Hot-&-sour Prawn Soup

Probably the best-known Thai soup, this is flavoured with lemon grass.

Serves 4–6

INGREDIENTS
450 g/1 lb raw king prawns
1 litre/1¾ pints/4 cups chicken stock or water
3 lemon grass stalks, bruised
10 kaffir lime leaves, torn in half
225 g/8 oz can straw mushrooms, drained
45 ml/3 tbsp fish sauce
50 ml/2 fl oz/¼ cup lime juice
30 ml/2 tbsp chopped spring onions
15 ml/1 tbsp fresh coriander leaves
4 red chillies, seeded and chopped

1 Shell and devein the prawns. Rinse the shells, place in a large saucepan with the stock or water and bring to the boil.

2 Add the lemon grass stalks to the stock with half the lime leaves. Simmer for 5–6 minutes until fragrant.

3 Strain the stock, return to the saucepan and reheat. Add the mushrooms and prawns, then cook until the prawns turn pink. Stir in the fish sauce, lime juice, spring onions, coriander, chillies and remaining lime leaves. Serve at once.

Right: Chicken & Coconut Soup (top);
Hot-&-sour Prawn Soup

Sweet-&-sour Fish

The sweet-and-sour sauce, with its colourful tomatoes, complements the strong flavour of the fish beautifully.

Serves 4–6

INGREDIENTS
1 large or 2 medium-size fish, such as
   snapper or mullet, cleaned and
   heads removed
20 ml/4 tsp cornflour
120 ml/4 fl oz/½ cup vegetable oil
15 ml/1 tbsp chopped garlic
15 ml/1 tbsp chopped fresh
   root ginger
30 ml/2 tbsp chopped shallots
225 g/8 oz cherry tomatoes
30 ml/2 tbsp red wine vinegar
30 ml/2 tbsp sugar
30 ml/2 tbsp tomato ketchup
15 ml/1 tbsp fish sauce
45 ml/3 tbsp water
salt and freshly ground black pepper
fresh coriander leaves and shredded spring
   onions, to garnish

1 Score the skin diagonally on both sides of the fish and coat lightly with 15 ml/1 tbsp of the cornflour.

2 Heat the oil in a wok or large frying pan and fry the fish for 6–7 minutes on both sides until it is crisp and brown. Transfer to a large serving platter and keep warm.

3 Pour off all but 30 ml/2 tbsp of the oil from the wok or pan and add the chopped garlic, ginger and shallots. Fry until golden, stirring frequently.

4 Add the cherry tomatoes and cook until they burst open. Stir in the red wine vinegar, sugar, tomato ketchup and fish sauce. Simmer the mixture gently for 1–2 minutes and adjust the seasoning according to taste.

5 Blend the remaining 5 ml/1 tsp cornflour with the water. Stir into the sauce and heat until it thickens, continuing to stir to prevent lumps forming. Pour the sauce over the fish, garnish with coriander and shredded spring onions and serve.

Steamed Fish with Chilli Sauce

Steaming is one of the best methods of cooking fish. Leave the fish whole and on the bone to retain all the flavour and moistness.

Serves 4

INGREDIENTS
1 large or 2 medium firm fish, such as
    bass or grouper, scaled and cleaned
2 banana leaves, or kitchen foil
30 ml/2 tbsp rice wine
3 red chillies, seeded and
    finely sliced
2 garlic cloves, finely chopped
2 cm/¾ in piece fresh root ginger,
    finely shredded
2 lemon grass stalks, bruised and
    finely chopped
2 spring onions, chopped
30 ml/2 tbsp fish sauce
juice of 1 lime

FOR THE CHILLI SAUCE
10 red chillies, seeded and chopped
4 garlic cloves, chopped
60 ml/4 tbsp fish sauce
15 ml/1 tbsp sugar
75 ml/5 tbsp lime juice

1 With a sharp knife, slash the skin of the fish a few times on both sides. Place the fish on a banana leaf or sheet of foil.

2 Mix together all the remaining ingredients and spread over surface of the fish.

3 Put a small, upturned plate in a wok and add 5 cm/2 in boiling water. Place the fish on the leaves or foil in the wok. Cover and steam for 10–15 minutes or until cooked.

4 Place all the chilli sauce ingredients in a food processor and process until smooth. You may need to add a little water if the sauce is too thick.

5 Serve the fish hot, on a banana leaf if liked, with the chilli sauce to spoon over the top.

Baked Fish in Banana Leaves

Fish that is prepared in this way is succulent and flavourful.

Serves 4

INGREDIENTS
250 ml/8 fl oz/1 cup coconut milk
30 ml/2 tbsp red curry paste
45 ml/3 tbsp fish sauce
30 ml/2 tbsp caster sugar
5 kaffir lime leaves, torn
4 x 175 g/6 oz fish fillets, such as snapper
175 g/6 oz mixed vegetables, such as carrots
   or leeks, finely shredded
4 banana leaves or kitchen foil
30 ml/2 tbsp shredded spring onions and
   2 red chillies, finely sliced, to garnish

1 Combine the coconut milk, curry paste, fish sauce, sugar and kaffir lime leaves in a shallow dish. Add the fish fillets and allow to marinate for 15–30 minutes. Preheat the oven to 200°C/400°F/Gas 6.

2 Lay some vegetables on a banana leaf or sheet of kitchen foil. Place a piece of fish on top with a little of its marinade. Wrap up by turning in the sides and ends of the leaf or foil and secure with cocktail sticks. Repeat with the rest of the leaves and fish.

3 Bake for 20–25 minutes or until cooked. Garnish with spring onions and red chillies.

Stir-fried Scallops

Asparagus and scallops are perfect partners in flavour and texture.

Serves 4–6

INGREDIENTS
60 ml/4 tbsp vegetable oil
1 bunch asparagus, cut into 5 cm/
   2 in lengths
4 garlic cloves, finely chopped
2 shallots, finely chopped
450 g/1 lb scallops, cleaned
30 ml/2 tbsp fish sauce
2.5 ml/½ tsp coarsely ground black pepper
120 ml/4 fl oz/½ cup coconut milk
fresh coriander leaves, to garnish

1 Heat half the oil in a wok or large frying pan. Add the asparagus and stir-fry for about 2 minutes. Transfer to a plate and set aside.

2 Add the rest of the oil, the garlic and shallots to the same wok and fry until fragrant. Add the scallops and cook for another 1–2 minutes.

3 Return the asparagus to the wok. Add the fish sauce, black pepper and coconut milk. Stir and cook for another 3–4 minutes or until the scallops and asparagus are cooked. Garnish with coriander and serve.

Right: Baked Fish in Banana Leaves (top); Stir-fried Scallops

Satay Prawns

An enticing and tasty dish. Serve with greens and jasmine rice.

Serves 4–6

INGREDIENTS
450 g/1 lb raw king prawns, shelled, tails left
   intact, and deveined
fresh coriander leaves, 4 red chillies, finely
   sliced, and spring onions, cut diagonally,
   to garnish

FOR THE PEANUT SAUCE
45 ml/3 tbsp vegetable oil
15 ml/1 tbsp chopped garlic
1 small onion, chopped
3–4 red chillies, crushed and chopped
3 kaffir lime leaves, torn
1 lemon grass stalk, bruised
   and chopped
5 ml/1 tsp medium curry paste
250 ml/8 fl oz/1 cup coconut milk
1 cm/½ in cinnamon stick
75 g/3 oz/⅓ cup crunchy peanut butter
45 ml/3 tbsp tamarind juice
30 ml/2 tbsp fish sauce
30 ml/2 tbsp palm sugar or soft dark
   brown sugar
juice of ½ lemon

1 To make the sauce, heat half the oil in a wok or large frying pan and add the chopped garlic and onion. Cook for 3–4 minutes, stirring, until the onion is soft.

2 Add the chillies, kaffir lime leaves, lemon grass and curry paste. Cook for a further 2–3 minutes.

3 Stir in the coconut milk, cinnamon stick, peanut butter, tamarind juice, fish sauce, sugar and lemon juice.

4 Reduce the heat and simmer gently for 15–20 minutes until the sauce thickens, stirring occasionally.

COOK'S TIP: Commercially made curry paste has a far superior flavour to curry powder. Once opened, it should be kept in the fridge and used within 2 months.

5 Heat the remaining oil in a separate wok or large frying pan. Add the prawns and stir-fry for 3–4 minutes or until they turn pink and are slightly firm to the touch.

6 Mix the prawns with the prepared sauce. Serve garnished with fresh coriander leaves, sliced red chillies and spring onions.

Stir-fried Prawns with Tamarind

The sour, tangy flavour that is characteristic of many Thai dishes comes from tamarind, a tropical fruit that resembles a bean pod.

Serves 4–6

INGREDIENTS
50 g/2 oz tamarind paste
150 ml/¼ pint/⅔ cup
   boiling water
30 ml/2 tbsp vegetable oil
30 ml/2 tbsp chopped onion
30 ml/2 tbsp palm sugar or soft dark
   brown sugar
30 ml/2 tbsp chicken stock
   or water
15 ml/1 tbsp fish sauce
6 dried red chillies, fried
450 g/1 lb raw shelled prawns
15 ml/1 tbsp fried chopped garlic
30 ml/2 tbsp fried sliced shallots
2 spring onions, chopped,
   to garnish

1 Put the tamarind paste in a small bowl, pour over the boiling water and stir well to break up any lumps. Leave for 30 minutes. Strain, pushing as much of the juice through as possible. Measure 90 ml/6 tbsp of the juice, the amount needed, and store the remainder in the fridge.

2 Heat the oil in a wok or large frying pan. Add the chopped onion and fry until golden brown, stirring occasionally to prevent sticking.

3 Add the sugar, chicken stock or water, fish sauce, fried chillies and the prepared tamarind juice, stirring well until the sugar dissolves. Bring the mixture to the boil.

4 Add the prawns, the fried garlic and shallots. Stir-fry for 3–4 minutes until the prawns are cooked. Garnish with the chopped spring onions and serve immediately.

Stir-fried Chicken with Basil & Chillies

This quick and easy chicken dish is an excellent introduction to Thai cuisine. Deep frying the basil adds another dimension to the dish.

Serves 4–6

INGREDIENTS
45 ml/3 tbsp vegetable oil
4 garlic cloves, sliced
2–4 red chillies, seeded
  and chopped
450 g/1 lb chicken, cut into
  bite-size pieces
30–45 ml/2–3 tbsp fish sauce
10 ml/2 tsp dark soy sauce
5 ml/1 tsp sugar
10–12 fresh Thai basil leaves
2 red chillies, finely sliced,
  to garnish
20 fresh Thai basil leaves,
  deep fried (optional)

2 Add the chicken and stir-fry until it changes colour. Add the fish sauce, dark soy sauce and sugar. Stir-fry for 3–4 minutes or until cooked through.

3 Stir in the fresh Thai basil leaves. Garnish with sliced chillies and the deep fried basil, if using, and serve.

COOK'S TIP: Thai basil leaves take only 30–40 seconds to deep fry.

1 Heat the oil in a wok or large frying pan over a high heat and swirl it around. Add the garlic and chillies and stir-fry for about 30 seconds until golden.

Red Chicken Curry with Bamboo Shoots

Bamboo shoots have a lovely, crunchy texture. It is quite acceptable to use canned bamboo, as fresh bamboo is not readily available in the West.

Serves 4–6

INGREDIENTS
1 litre/1¾ pints/4 cups coconut milk
30 ml/2 tbsp red curry paste
450 g/1 lb diced boneless chicken
30 ml/2 tbsp fish sauce
15 ml/1 tbsp sugar
225 g/8 oz bamboo shoots,
    rinsed and sliced
5 kaffir lime leaves, torn
salt and freshly ground black pepper
2 red chillies, seeded and chopped,
    10–12 fresh basil leaves and
    10–12 fresh mint leaves, to garnish

1 In a large, heavy-based saucepan, bring half the coconut milk to the boil, stirring until it separates.

3 Add the chicken, fish sauce and sugar. Fry for 3–5 minutes until the chicken changes colour, stirring constantly to prevent it from sticking to the base of the pan.

2 Add 30 ml/2 tbsp of the red curry paste and cook for a few minutes, stirring to blend it with the milk.

4 Add the rest of the coconut milk, the bamboo shoots and kaffir lime leaves. Bring back to the boil. Adjust the seasoning to taste. Serve garnished with chopped red chillies and fresh basil and mint leaves.

Sweet-&-sour Pork

Sweet-and-sour is traditionally a Chinese creation, but the Thais do it very well. This version has an altogether fresher and cleaner flavour.

Serves 4

INGREDIENTS
350 g/12 oz lean pork
30 ml/2 tbsp vegetable oil
4 garlic cloves, finely sliced
1 small red onion, sliced
30 ml/2 tbsp fish sauce
15 ml/1 tbsp sugar
1 red pepper, seeded and diced
½ cucumber, seeded and sliced lengthways
2 plum tomatoes, cut into wedges
115 g/4 oz pineapple, cut into small chunks
2 spring onions, cut into short lengths
freshly ground black pepper
fresh coriander leaves and shredded spring onions, to garnish

1 Slice the pork into thin strips. Heat the oil in a wok or large frying pan and swirl it around.

2 Add the garlic and fry until golden, then add the pork and stir-fry for 4–5 minutes. Add the onion.

3 Season with the fish sauce, sugar and freshly ground black pepper. Stir to ensure well combined and continue cooking for 3–4 minutes, or until the pork is cooked through.

4 Add the diced red pepper, sliced cucumber, wedges of tomato, pineapple chunks and spring onions. You may need to add a few table-spoons of water if the mixture seems dry. Continue to stir-fry the mixture for another 3–4 minutes. Serve hot garnished with fresh coriander leaves and shredded spring onions.

Special Chow Mein

The *lap cheong* used in this recipe is an air-dried Chinese sausage, available from most Chinese supermarkets. If you find it difficult to obtain, it may be replaced with diced ham, chorizo or salami.

Serves 4–6

INGREDIENTS
45 ml/3 tbsp vegetable oil
2 garlic cloves, sliced
5 ml/1 tsp chopped fresh
    root ginger
2 red chillies, seeded and chopped
2 *lap cheong*, about 75 g/3 oz, rinsed and
    sliced (optional)
1 boneless chicken breast, thinly sliced
16 raw tiger prawns, shelled, tails left
    intact, and deveined
115 g/4 oz green beans
225 g/8 oz beansprouts
50 g/2 oz garlic chives
450 g/1 lb egg noodles, cooked in boiling
    water until tender
30 ml/2 tbsp soy sauce
15 ml/1 tbsp oyster sauce
15 ml/1 tbsp sesame oil
salt and freshly ground black pepper
2 spring onions, shredded, and
    15 ml/1 tbsp fresh coriander leaves,
    to garnish

1 Heat 15 ml/1 tbsp of the oil in a wok or large frying pan and fry the garlic, ginger and chillies. Add the *lap cheong*, if using, and the chicken, prawns and beans. Stir-fry over a high heat for about 2 minutes or until the chicken and prawns are cooked. Transfer to a bowl and set aside.

2 Heat the rest of the oil in the same wok. Add the beansprouts and garlic chives. Stir-fry for 1–2 minutes.

3 Add the egg noodles and toss and stir to mix. Season to taste with soy sauce, oyster sauce, salt and pepper.

4 Return the prawn mixture to the wok. Reheat and mix well with the noodles. Stir in the sesame oil. Serve garnished with spring onions and coriander leaves.

Stir-fried Beef in Oyster Sauce

A simple but delicious recipe, using several types of mushroom.

Serves 4–6

INGREDIENTS
450 g/1 lb rump steak
30 ml/2 tbsp soy sauce
15 ml/1 tbsp cornflour
45 ml/3 tbsp vegetable oil
15 ml/1 tbsp chopped garlic
15 ml/1 tbsp chopped fresh
    root ginger
225 g/8 oz mixed mushrooms, such as
    shiitake, oyster and straw
30 ml/2 tbsp oyster sauce
5 ml/1 tsp sugar
4 spring onions, cut into short lengths
freshly ground black pepper
2 red chillies, seeded and cut into strips,
    to garnish

1 Slice the beef, on the diagonal, into long, thin strips. Mix together the soy sauce and cornflour in a large bowl, stir in the beef and leave to marinate for 1–2 hours.

2 Heat half the oil in a wok or frying pan. Add the garlic and ginger and fry until fragrant. Stir in the beef. Stir to separate the strips, let them colour and cook for 1–2 minutes. Remove from the pan and set aside.

3 Heat the remaining oil in the wok. Add the shiitake, oyster and straw mushrooms. Cook until tender.

4 Return the beef to the wok with the mushrooms. Add the oyster sauce, sugar and freshly ground black pepper to taste. Mix well, then add the spring onions. Serve garnished with strips of red chilli.

COOK'S TIP: Made from extracts of oysters, oyster sauce is velvety smooth and has a savoury/sweet and meaty taste. There are several types available; buy the best you can afford.

Green Beef Curry with Thai Aubergine

This is a very quick curry, so be sure to use good quality meat.

Serves 4–6

INGREDIENTS
15 ml/1 tbsp vegetable oil
45 ml/3 tbsp green curry paste
600 ml/1 pint/2½ cups
    coconut milk
450 g/1 lb beef sirloin, cut into
    long, thin slices
4 kaffir lime leaves, torn
15–30 ml/1–2 tbsp fish sauce
5 ml/1 tsp palm sugar or soft dark
    brown sugar
150 g/5 oz small Thai
    aubergines, halved
a small handful of fresh
    Thai basil
2 green chillies, finely shredded,
    to garnish

2 Gradually stir in half the coconut milk. Cook for about 5–6 minutes, until an oily sheen appears.

3 Add the slices of beef to the saucepan with the kaffir lime leaves, fish sauce, sugar and halved aubergines. Cook for 2–3 minutes, then stir in the remaining coconut milk.

1 Heat the oil in a large saucepan or wok. Add the green curry paste and fry until fragrant, stirring constantly to avoid sticking.

4 Bring back to a simmer and cook until the meat and aubergines are tender. Stir in the Thai basil just before serving, and garnish with green chillies.

Thick Beef Curry in Sweet Peanut Sauce

This curry is deliciously rich and thicker than most other Thai curries. Serve with boiled jasmine rice and salted duck's eggs, if liked.

Serves 4–6

INGREDIENTS
600 ml/1 pint/2½ cups coconut milk
45 ml/3 tbsp red curry paste
45 ml/3 tbsp fish sauce
30 ml/2 tbsp palm sugar or soft dark
   brown sugar
2 lemon grass stalks, bruised
450 g/1 lb rump steak, cut into thin strips
75 g/3 oz/¾ cup roasted ground peanuts
2 red chillies, seeded and sliced
5 kaffir lime leaves, torn
salt and freshly ground black pepper
10–15 fresh Thai basil leaves, to garnish
2 salted duck's eggs, to serve (optional)

3 Continue to cook until the colour deepens. Add the rest of the coconut milk and stir to combine. Bring the mixture back to the boil.

1 Put half the coconut milk into a heavy-based saucepan and heat, stirring, until it boils and separates.

2 Add the red curry paste and cook until fragrant. Add the fish sauce, sugar and lemon grass.

4 Add the strips of beef and the ground peanuts. Stir and leave to cook for 8–10 minutes or until most of the liquid in the pan has evaporated.

5 Add the chillies and kaffir lime leaves. Adjust the seasoning to taste. Garnish with Thai basil leaves and serve with salted eggs, if using.

Water Spinach with Brown Bean Sauce

Water spinach, or Siamese watercress, has arrowhead leaves.

Serves 4–6

INGREDIENTS
1 bunch water spinach, about
    1 kg/2¼ lb in weight
45 ml/3 tbsp vegetable oil
15 ml/1 tbsp chopped garlic
15 ml/1 tbsp brown bean sauce
30 ml/2 tbsp fish sauce
15 ml/1 tbsp sugar
freshly ground black pepper

1 Trim and discard the bottom, coarse, woody end of the water spinach. Cut the remaining part into 5 cm/2 in lengths, keeping the leaves separate from the stems.

2 Heat the oil in a wok or large frying pan. Add the chopped garlic and toss for 10 seconds. Add the stem part of the water spinach, let it sizzle and cook for 1 minute, then add the leafy parts.

3 Add the brown bean sauce, fish sauce, sugar and freshly ground black pepper, and stir well to combine. Toss and turn over the spinach for about 3–4 minutes until it begins to wilt. Serve immediately.

Mixed Vegetables in Coconut Milk

Coconut milk adds richness to the vegetables without masking them.

Serves 4–6

INGREDIENTS
450 g/1 lb mixed vegetables, such as
    aubergines, baby sweetcorn, carrots,
    asparagus and patty pan squash
8 red chillies, seeded
2 lemon grass stalks, chopped
4 kaffir lime leaves, torn
30 ml/2 tbsp vegetable oil
250 ml/8 fl oz/1 cup coconut milk
30 ml/2 tbsp fish sauce
salt
15–20 fresh Thai basil leaves, to garnish

1 Cut the vegetables into similar-size shapes. Put the chillies, lemon grass and kaffir lime leaves in a mortar and grind together. Heat the oil in a wok or large frying pan. Add the chilli mixture and fry for 2–3 minutes.

2 Stir in the coconut milk and bring to the boil. Add the vegetables and cook for about 5 minutes. Season with the fish sauce and salt. Garnish with fresh Thai basil leaves and serve.

Right: Water Spinach with Brown Bean Sauce (top); Mixed Vegetables in Coconut Milk

Beancurd & Green Bean Red Curry

This recipe uses green beans, but you can use almost any kind of vegetable such as aubergines, bamboo shoots or broccoli.

Serves 4–6

INGREDIENTS
600 ml/1 pint/2½ cups coconut milk
15 ml/1 tbsp red curry paste
45 ml/3 tbsp fish sauce
10 ml/2 tsp palm sugar or soft dark
   brown sugar
225 g/8 oz/3 cups button mushrooms
115 g/4 oz/1 cup green beans, trimmed
175 g/6 oz beancurd (tofu), rinsed and cut
   into 4 cm/1½ in cubes
4 kaffir lime leaves, torn
2 red chillies, sliced
fresh coriander leaves, to garnish

1 Cook one-third of the coconut milk in a wok or saucepan until it separates and an oily sheen appears.

2 Add the red curry paste, fish sauce and sugar to the coconut milk. Mix together thoroughly.

3 Add the button mushrooms. Stir and cook for 1 minute. Stir in the rest of the coconut milk and bring the mixture back to the boil.

4 Add the green beans and cubes of beancurd and simmer gently for another 4–5 minutes.

5 Stir in the torn kaffir lime leaves and the sliced red chillies. Serve the curry garnished with the fresh coriander leaves.

Jasmine Rice

This aromatic, long grain rice is the staple of most Thai meals.

Serves 4–6

INGREDIENTS
450 g/1 lb/2 cups jasmine rice
750 ml/1¼ pints/3 cups cold water

1 Rinse the rice thoroughly at least three times in cold water until the water runs clear.

2 Put the rice in a heavy-based saucepan and add the water. Bring to a vigorous boil, uncovered. Stir and reduce the heat to low. Cover and simmer for up to 20 minutes or until all the water has been absorbed. Remove from the heat and leave to stand for 10 minutes.

3 Remove the lid and stir the rice gently with a rice paddle or a pair of wooden chopsticks, to fluff up and separate the grains.

COOK'S TIP: An electric rice cooker cooks the rice and keeps it warm. Different sizes and models of rice cookers are available. The top of the range is a non-stick version, which is a little expensive, but well worth the investment.

Fried Jasmine Rice

The unique pungency of the basil gives this a special Thai flavour.

Serves 4–6

INGREDIENTS
45 ml/3 tbsp vegetable oil
1 egg, beaten
1 onion, chopped
15 ml/1 tbsp chopped garlic
15 ml/1 tbsp shrimp paste
1 kg/2¼ lb/4 cups cooked jasmine rice
350 g/12 oz cooked shelled prawns
50 g/2 oz thawed frozen peas
oyster sauce, to taste
2 spring onions, chopped
15–20 fresh Thai basil leaves, roughly
    snipped, plus an extra sprig, to garnish

1 Heat 15 ml/1 tbsp of the oil in a wok. Add the egg and swirl it around to make a thin pancake. Cook until golden, slide out, roll up and cut into thin strips. Set aside.

2 Heat the remaining oil and fry the onion and garlic for 2–3 minutes. Stir in the shrimp paste. Add the cooked jasmine rice, prawns and peas and stir until heated through.

3 Season with oyster sauce. Add the onions and basil. Serve topped with the pancake strips and a basil sprig.

Right: Jasmine Rice (top); Fried Jasmine Rice

Thai Fried Noodles

Made with rice noodles, this is considered one of the national dishes of Thailand and has a fascinating flavour and texture.

Serves 4–6

INGREDIENTS
45 ml/3 tbsp vegetable oil
15 ml/1 tbsp chopped garlic
16 raw king prawns, shells, tails left
    intact, and deveined
2 eggs, lightly beaten
15 ml/1 tbsp dried shrimps, rinsed
30 ml/2 tbsp pickled white radish
50 g/2 oz fried beancurd (tofu), cut into
    small slivers
2.5 ml/½ tsp dried chilli flakes
350 g/12 oz rice noodles, soaked in
    warm water for 20–30 minutes
    and drained
115 g/4 oz garlic chives, cut into
    5 cm/2 in lengths
225 g/8 oz beansprouts
50 g/2 oz/½ cup roasted peanuts,
    coarsely ground
5 ml/1 tsp sugar
15 ml/1 tbsp dark soy sauce
30 ml/2 tbsp fish sauce
30 ml/2 tbsp tamarind juice
30 ml/2 tbsp fresh coriander leaves
    and kaffir lime wedges,
    to garnish

1 Heat 15 ml/1 tbsp of the oil in a wok or large frying pan. Add the garlic and fry until golden. Stir in the king prawns and cook for 1–2 minutes until pink, tossing from time to time. Remove and set aside.

2 Heat another 15 ml/1 tbsp oil in the wok. Add the eggs and tilt the wok to spread them into a thin sheet. Stir to scramble and break the egg into small pieces. Remove from the wok and set aside with the prawns.

3 Heat the remaining oil in the wok. Add the dried shrimps, pickled radish, beancurd and chilli flakes. Stir briefly. Add the drained noodles and stir-fry for 5 minutes.

4 Add the garlic chives, half the beansprouts and half the roasted peanuts. Season with the sugar, soy sauce, fish sauce and tamarind juice. Mix well and continue to cook until the noodles are heated through.

5 Return the prawn and egg mixture to the wok and mix with the noodles. Serve garnished with the remaining beansprouts and peanuts, coriander leaves and lime wedges.

Crispy Fried Rice Vermicelli

This crisp tangle of fried rice vermicelli, tossed in a piquant garlic, sweet-and-sour sauce, is usually served at celebration meals.

Serves 4–6

INGREDIENTS
oil, for deep frying
175 g/6 oz rice vermicelli
15 ml/1 tbsp chopped garlic
4–6 dried chillies, seeded and chopped
30 ml/2 tbsp chopped shallot
15 ml/1 tbsp dried shrimps, rinsed
115 g/4 oz minced pork
115 g/4 oz raw shelled prawns, chopped
30 ml/2 tbsp brown bean sauce
30 ml/2 tbsp rice wine vinegar
45 ml/3 tbsp fish sauce
75 g/3 oz palm sugar or soft dark
    brown sugar
30 ml/2 tbsp tamarind or
    lime juice
115 g/4 oz beansprouts

FOR THE GARNISH
2 spring onions, shredded
30 ml/2 tbsp fresh coriander leaves
2 heads pickled garlic (optional)
2-egg omelette, rolled and sliced
2 red chillies, seeded
    and chopped

1 Heat the oil in a wok. Break the vermicelli into small handfuls about 7.5 cm/3 in long. Deep fry in the hot oil until they puff up. Remove and drain on kitchen paper.

2 Leave 30 ml/2 tbsp of the oil in the wok, add the garlic, chillies, shallot and dried shrimps and fry until fragrant. Add the minced pork and stir-fry for 3–4 minutes until it is no longer pink. Add the chopped prawns and fry for 2 minutes. Remove the mixture from the wok and set aside.

3 To the same wok, add the brown bean sauce, rice wine vinegar, fish sauce and sugar. Bring to a gentle boil, stir to dissolve the sugar and continue to cook until syrupy.

4 Add the tamarind or lime juice to the wok and adjust the seasoning to taste. The sauce should be sweet, sour and salty. Reduce the heat.

5 Add the pork mixture and the beansprouts to the sauce in the wok and stir to coat well.

6 Add the rice vermicelli to the wok and toss gently to coat with the sauce without breaking the vermicelli too much.

7 Transfer the vermicelli to a warmed serving platter and garnish with shredded spring onions, coriander, pickled garlic (if liked), omelette strips and red chillies. Serve immediately.

55

Seafood Salad with Herbs

A fragrant and nourishing dish.

Serves 4–6

INGREDIENTS
250 ml/8 fl oz/1 cup fish stock or water
350 g/12 oz squid, cleaned and cut into rings
12 raw king prawns, shelled
12 scallops
50 g/2 oz bean thread noodles, soaked in
    warm water for 30 minutes
½ cucumber, cut into thin sticks
1 lemon grass stalk, finely chopped
2 kaffir lime leaves, finely shredded
2 shallots, finely sliced
juice of 1–2 limes
30 ml/2 tbsp fish sauce
30 ml/2 tbsp chopped spring onion
30 ml/2 tbsp fresh coriander leaves
12–15 fresh mint leaves, roughly torn
4 red chillies, sliced
fresh coriander sprigs, to garnish

1 Pour the stock or water into a medium-size saucepan, set over a high heat and bring to the boil. Cook each type of seafood separately for a few minutes. Drain and set aside.

2 Drain the noodles and cut into pieces about 5 cm/2 in long. Combine with the cooked seafood.

3 Add all the remaining ingredients, mix together well and serve garnished with the coriander sprigs.

Pomelo Salad

A pomelo resembles a grapefruit.

Serves 4–6

INGREDIENTS
30 ml/2 tbsp vegetable oil
4 shallots, finely sliced
2 garlic cloves, finely sliced
1 large pomelo
115 g/4 oz cooked shelled prawns
115 g/4 oz cooked crab meat
15 ml/1 tbsp roasted peanuts, ground
10–12 small fresh mint leaves
2 spring onions, finely sliced
2 red chillies, seeded and finely sliced
fresh coriander leaves
shredded fresh coconut (optional)

FOR THE DRESSING
30 ml/2 tbsp fish sauce
15 ml/1 tbsp palm sugar or soft
    dark brown sugar
30 ml/2 tbsp lime juice

1 Whisk together the dressing ingredients and set aside. Fry the shallots and garlic in the oil until golden and set aside.

2 Combine small pieces of pomelo with prawns, crab, peanuts, mint and shallot mixture. Dress the salad and sprinkle over the remaining ingredients.

Right: Seafood Salad with Herbs (top);
Pomelo Salad

Tapioca Pudding

Lychees or the smaller, similar-tasting logans go well with this.

Serves 4

INGREDIENTS
115 g/4 oz/⅔ cup tapioca
475 ml/16 fl oz/2 cups water
175 g/6 oz sugar
250 ml/8 fl oz/1 cup coconut milk
pinch of salt
finely shredded rind of 1 lime, to decorate
250 g/9 oz prepared tropical fruits,
    to serve

1 Soak the tapioca in warm water for about 1 hour to swell. Drain thoroughly. Bring the water to the boil in a saucepan. Stir in the sugar and salt. Add the tapioca and coconut milk and simmer for 10 minutes or until the tapioca turns transparent.

2 Serve warm accompanied by tropical fruits and decorated with fine shreds of lime rind.

Fried Bananas

These delicious treats are sold at roadside stalls in Thailand.

Serves 4

INGREDIENTS
115 g/4 oz/1 cup plain flour
2.5 ml/½ tsp bicarbonate of soda
30 ml/2 tbsp sugar
1 egg
90 ml/6 tbsp water
30 ml/2 tbsp shredded coconut or
    15 ml/1 tbsp sesame seeds
4 firm bananas, peeled
oil, for frying
pinch of salt
fresh mint sprigs and fresh lychees,
    to decorate
30 ml/2 tbsp honey, to serve (optional)

1 Sift the flour, bicarbonate of soda and salt into a bowl. Stir in the sugar. Whisk in the egg and enough water to make a thin batter. Whisk in the coconut or sesame seeds.

2 Cut each banana in half lengthways and crossways. Dip in the batter, then fry in hot oil until golden brown.

3 Remove from the oil and drain on kitchen paper. Decorate with mint and lychees and serve with honey, if using.

Right: Tapioca Pudding (top);
Fried Bananas

Coconut Custard

This traditional dish can be baked or steamed and is often served with sweet sticky rice and a selection of fruit such as mango and tamarillo.

Serves 4–6

INGREDIENTS

4 eggs
75 g/3 oz soft light brown sugar
250 ml/8 fl oz/1 cup coconut milk
5 ml/1 tsp vanilla, rose or
    jasmine extract
fresh mint leaves and icing sugar,
    to decorate
prepared tropical fruits,
    to serve

2 Strain the mixture and pour into individual ramekins. Stand the ramekins in a roasting tin. Pour hot water into the tin to reach halfway up the outsides of the ramekins.

1 Preheat the oven to 150°C/300°F/ Gas 2. Whisk the eggs and sugar in a bowl until smooth. Add the coconut milk and vanilla, rose or jasmine extract and continue to whisk to ensure that they are well blended.

VARIATION: If tropical fruits are not in season you could substitute strawberries, pears or peaches.

3 Bake for about 35–40 minutes or until the custards are set. Test with a fine skewer or cocktail stick. Remove from the oven and leave to cool.

4 Turn out on to a plate, and surround with fruit. Decorate with mint leaves and icing sugar and serve.

Baked Rice Pudding

Black sticky rice gives this baked pudding a distinct character and an unusual nutty flavour.

Serves 4–6

INGREDIENTS
175 g/6 oz/³⁄₄ cup white or black
    sticky rice
30 ml/2 tbsp soft light
    brown sugar
250 ml/8 fl oz/1 cup water
475 ml/16 fl oz/2 cups coconut milk
3 eggs
30 ml/2 tbsp sugar

1 Put the rice, sugar, water and half the coconut milk in a saucepan. Bring the mixture to the boil and simmer for 15–20 minutes or until the rice has absorbed most of the liquid, stirring occasionally. Preheat the oven to 150°C/300°F/Gas 2.

2 Transfer the rice into an ovenproof dish. Mix together the eggs, remaining coconut milk and sugar in a bowl. Strain and pour evenly over the par-boiled rice.

3 Place the dish in a roasting tin. Pour in enough boiling water to come halfway up the sides of the dish. Cover the dish with foil and bake for about 35 minutes–1 hour or until the custard is set. Serve warm or cold.

Mango with Sticky Rice

Mangoes, with their delicate fragrance, blend especially well with coconut sticky rice.

Serves 4

INGREDIENTS
115 g/4 oz sticky white rice, washed and
    soaked in water overnight
175 ml/6 fl oz/³⁄₄ cup thick coconut milk
45 ml/3 tbsp sugar
2 ripe mangoes, peeled, stoned and sliced
pinch of salt
strips of lime rind, to decorate

1 Drain the rice and spread in an even layer in a steamer lined with muslin. Cover and steam for about 20 minutes or until tender.

2 Meanwhile, reserve 45 ml/3 tbsp of the top of the coconut milk and combine the rest with the sugar and salt in a pan. Bring to the boil, stirring until the sugar dissolves, then pour into a bowl to cool a little.

3 Turn the rice into a bowl and pour over the coconut mixture. Stir, then leave for about 10–15 minutes. To serve, place the mangoes on top of the rice and drizzle over the reserved coconut milk. Decorate with lime rind.

Right: Baked Rice Pudding (top);
Mango with Sticky Rice